MY SUITE A$$!

Surviving: Chaos, Critics & Crazies

TAMMY MAYHEW

ISBN 978-1-7342552-0-1 (Print)
ISBN 978-1-7342552-1-8 (eBook)

Cover design & book design by Noah Adam Paperman
Cover photo & author photo courtesy of CodieBEAUCreative

Publisher's Cataloging-in-Publication Data
provided by Five Rainbows Cataloging Services

Names: Mayhew, Tammy, author.
Title: My suite a$$! : surviving : chaos, critics & crazies / Tammy Mayhew.
Description: Safford, AZ : CCC LLC, 2020.
Identifiers: ISBN 978-1-7342552-0-1 (paperback) | ISBN 978-1-7342552-1-8 (ebook)
Subjects: LCSH: Hotels--Employees. | Hotels--Anecdotes. | Hotel clerks. | Customer relations. | Businesswomen. | Entrepreneurship. | Wit and humor. | BISAC: BUSINESS & ECONOMICS / Industries / Hospitality, Travel & Tourism. | BUSINESS & ECONOMICS / Customer Relations. | HUMOR / Topic / Business & Professional.
Classification: LCC TX911.3.F75 M39 2020 (print) | LCC TX911.3.F75 (ebook) | DDC 647.94--dc23.

Thank you to all the wonderfully amazing customers that have kept me in this industry for so many years. They are truly the reason I stayed in it this long. The sweet patrons and the dedicated and inspiring team of people I had the privilege of working with and serving for so many years, and my steadfastly supportive family are the reasons I am not in prison. Kudos to the local townspeople who, when they heard my stories, told me I should write a book because it would make a great read for the shitter. It is by the grace of God and family that I never had to hire an attorney or be bailed out of jail, after dealing with the rest.

Table of Contents

Introduction

Translation: Who the hell am I and why should you give a shit?

That is what all those damn advice books should say when they introduce the author, guru, life coach or whatever other over-inflated, egotistical, narcissistic title they want to give themselves. They spend half the book listing varied degrees and their many rose-colored accolades, mindlessly justifying why you should listen to them at all, citing overused advice and sugar-coated anecdotes from Confucius to Gandhi. Nope, I am just me, and according to the U.S. Department of Labor, that means I am just like the tens of millions of you.

Don't worry, I'm not about to get all warm and fuzzy on you or think we are some new age tribe just because so many of us have, at one time or another, worked in the customer service industry. You know...flipping burgers, waiting tables, bartending, sales, retail, front desk, housekeeper, dishwasher, pool boy, concierge, busser, customer service rep, and actually... yes—I have done all of those jobs during my career, and a few others, to boot.

Look, we all start out in these jobs for a multitude of reasons: our first job, working our way through school, making ends meet, and yes, some even do make it a career. Lord knows I did. For the others that did, this book is for you, and my hats off to you. Just curious as to how many of you are currently or have been in therapy?

I was pretty much born into it when my parents decided to sell everything they owned except what would fit into an old but faithful two-tone green and white Dodge Travco motorhome, and moved themselves and their four kids across country to own a condemned mom-and-pop motel in rural Arizona. I was a tenderly naive ten-year-old girl when this adventure began. To be exact, it was May of 1976 and I wondered what alien life force had possessed my stoic hard-working parents to leave the cool and seasonal North and our large family in Michigan and Wisconsin and move to HOT, desolate, rural, Southern Arizona, where we knew no one.

It might have been or should have been an omen when we saw that the highway that took us into our new hometown was Highway 666. God's honest truth—the devil's highway. Can anyone say, Big Giant Red Flag? When we got to this new adventure our parents, rightfully, wouldn't even let us stay in the house that doubled as a front desk office and laundry room until we cleaned it thoroughly. The house was complete with a now vintage rotary dial headset switchboard with grimy red braided lines that plugged into the metal lined holes, portals where we could listen in on guests' lives by just turning the little black switch. Not saying we ever did, just that we could. But wait, you're probably wondering, if it was a motel, couldn't we have stayed in one or two of the cozy little casita rooms? You would think so, but no. The house was bad, but the rooms were worse. It was a thirty-six-unit casita-style motel with weeping mortar dripping out in a kaleidoscope of blue, green and gold that marked, like tree rings, the more than thirty years since it had been built and the times it was painted.

The rooms smelled of the sickly sweet, stagnant, sweaty smell of too many guests and not enough bleach and elbow grease. We had been told that there was a pool and swaying palm trees, which led us children to wistfully dream of an idle tropical paradise where we would swim and laugh and sip cold refreshing little pineapple umbrella drinks.

That may have eventually come to fruition, minus the foo foo drinks, but first that kidney shaped pool had to be found under the dry desert dirt, dug out, cleaned, painted, filled and fenced. The place was like an eerie, seething, dusty cross between *Psycho* and *The Shining*. There was a hell of a lot of work to be done before we could even leave the safety and security of that little olive-green fiberglass box on wheels.

Our family was no stranger to hard work, and we looked at it through the eyes of adventurers and explorers. Just opening the door of every room was a new and disgusting experience. There were rancid musty smells and mysterious sticky stains. It took us all of two weeks to get everything clean enough for my mom to be okay with us moving in. The pool took a bit longer.

It has taken more than forty years of innovations and varying job titles, from switchboards to PBX phone systems, from staying up all night looking out a window to handheld video surveillance, from cleaning rooms and pools to working the front desk or counter, to gain my knowledge and experience. Mix all of that with a wonderful husband of thirty-five years (no kidding, same man. and I still adore him), three kids, seven grandbabies, four more hotels, two restaurants, a convention center and a gift shop later, and I feel I am more than qualified to write this story. Oh, and a stint at managing a two-state garbage company while still taking care of the mom-and-pop.

I didn't grow up in a bad place—quite the contrary. The small town in Arizona was hotter than hell, and I really don't give a shit for the "but it's a dry heat" crap—it was just fucking hot. The valley was thickly intertwined with families growing bigger by the minute. If you weren't Mormon, then you were Catholic, and we all know they both believe in large families. No greater purpose in life than procreation. This, combined with the fact that the county didn't get cable until the eighties, meant lots of kids.

Everyone knew or was related to everyone else. Dating was like playing the genetics lottery or DNA Russian Roulette. A game of who are your parents, grandparents, aunts and uncles......*shit*, we're related; next. Albeit I was only ten when we moved there, it still meant there was potential for dating for all of us some day. You know, mix up the gene pool. Making that a little tougher though was the fact that we were white and not Mormon, and Catholic but not Hispanic.

A beautifully rugged ten-thousand-foot mountain stood majestically just outside our door, that helped paint some of the most tear-worthy skies I have ever seen. Colors so vivid it seemed like a painted backdrop from a movie scene. It was like the hand of God scattered the width and breadth of the skies with a vibrant varied pallet of oranges, yellows, pinks, purples and blues. The pace was slower compared to Milwaukee—understatement of my life—with the quintessential main street, full of family-owned stores standing shoulder to shoulder. It was lined with charming shops manned by honest folks selling their talents and wares. Everyone knew who did what.

There was the shoe repair shop, where skilled men with hands as worn and tough as the leather they worked on still repaired your shoes and boots, because you just didn't throw something away when it was worn or broken. You fixed it and gave it new life. There was one photographer in town, and he was good, and one dry cleaner, and he was dependable. They had to be, because on Sunday they, like their stores, would be sitting shoulder to shoulder sharing pews with those they served and did business with.

There was the office supply store, whose grey-haired, bespectacled owner limped from surviving polio, the department store run by a great little reserved couple that were holocaust survivors, the parts store that didn't have to ask the make and model of your car because they already knew what you drove. The pharmacy where you sat at the old-fashioned, intricately carved solid wood soda fountain while they filled your prescription and you satisfied your sweet tooth on those stifling hot days with a cold old-fashioned soda or creamy melting homemade ice cream. Lastly the sturdy towering brick courthouse loomed at the end of main street, standing as a staunch and constant reminder to all who walked that quaint little street that law, and order would prevail. No kidding, I really grew up there. Mayberry had nothing on us.

There were the town characters that everyone knew. The man who always rode his mule into town and would stop and give my kids rides with a smile. Didn't matter that he had once killed a man. The small-town grapevine said the other man should have left him alone in that bar, and when he wouldn't, he made sure that man wouldn't bother him or anyone else ever again. I figured the story had to be true, as he was a tall lanky African American man who had shot and killed a white man in the sixties and had not been prosecuted, as the town and bar patrons stood behind his word.

He would drive around in his little steampunk—before it was popular—truck that could extend a ladder to trim palm trees or attach a shaker and shake the meat out of your pecan trees. Never heard an unkind word from his mouth, nothing but a crooked smile and a hearty laugh. I saw him limping one day and asked him what was wrong. He told me his stubborn old mule had fallen, with him on it, and broke his foot.

Foolishly and with genuine concern, I asked him if he had gone to the doctor. That sweet crooked grin came out as he stroked the coat of his sweaty mule, and he looked down at me with a twinkle in his eye and said, "Now why would I do that? I know it's broke. Not gonna pay good money to a doctor to tell me that? I just put my boot on and will leave it on for a month or two and it will be just fine." Couldn't argue with that logic or that smile.

Then there was a giant of a man, both in stature and in heart. He owned the local towing company and was every inch of seven feet tall and over three hundred pounds of pure kindness. Legend had it that he could pick up the end of a car and move it wherever it needed to be. His hands were the only ones I ever saw swallow my daddy's hands completely. If you asked him if he went to college, he would nod and tell you he went through it.

No surprise he had been offered a "full" scholarship to play football at the local community college, and the well-intentioned coach told him he wouldn't have to pay for anything. Great, even though he was a steadfastly gentle soul, he would do it. He eagerly went to register for his classes, and they said everything was covered, but he would need to buy a drafting set. A resounding but quiet *No* was his answer. It was his understanding that everything would be paid for. They told him yes, but not the drafting set. He kindly bid them good day and went to visit with the coach and told him what was going on and waited patiently for his reply. Coach made a few phone calls and then told him that yes, he would have to buy the drafting set. He stood up shook the coach's hand and promptly left and didn't come back. So, he always said he went through college...in the front door and out the back.

You can see I was raised among hardworking, honest, resourceful folks. Faithful people who did business with you on a firm handshake and they expected the same. Everyone was as good as their word and family name, so they took care of both. I grew up with a lot of really great people.... reliable, modest and humble farmers, ranchers, miners and prison guards. Yes, we laid claim to being the home of three prisons— two state and one federal. Hell, we even housed a Watergate felon.

This type of upbringing raises you up right but gives you short patience when it comes to whiners. Now don't get me wrong, there is a way to constructively complain when there's a legitimate issue and, in that case, I have all the patience and sympathy in the world and will do everything within my power to make it right. After all, that's how I was raised, and I took great pride in that.

But then there are the whiners, chronic complainers, deflectors and just plain jackasses. We all know them. Liars, con artists and the completely insatiable folks that would complain if you wiped their ass with solid gold toilet paper. The shame of these unquenchable sociopathic asshole customers is they make up less than one percent of your customer base— that is, if you are doing your job right. You would think that with numbers like that you would better remember all the wonderful customers. But no, our minds just don't work that way.

Instead we remember the other less than one percent of psychos and morons. I realize I'm probably not being politically correct here, with the word "psychos." All I have to say about that is judge me after you read the book and then feel free to write me a "strongly worded letter" and suggest another less offensive, politically correct, snowflake-approved term that fits the story.

I am just telling the story we all want to tell, the way we want to honestly tell it, with no sugar coating, and hope those less-than-one-percenters read it, recognize themselves and either change the way they interact with people or by all means, be my guest and FUCK the HELL OFF!

Hah, you know it felt good to read that, and let me tell you, it felt great to write it. Go ahead, before you turn the page, yell it from the roof tops......just not at work, school, church or in front of your in-laws, unless you are quitting, graduating or getting divorced.

You can take this book as a lesson or a warning, your book, your experience, your choice. But know this, I have sugar-coated more bullshit responses to unfounded customer complaints and infuriating customer behavior than this one book can possibly ever contain.

THERE WAS NO _I_ IN MY INTRODUCTION

(SO HERE I AM)

I am notoriously bad at letting people in. I think this is very often the case with many of us lifelong Service Warriors I wanted this book to be a look at the humorous side of it all, something not quite so serious. A way to gain some insight without the classroom monotony. It is said that humor masks the troubled heart and keeps the soul from dying. See, now that doesn't sound quite as hilarious as the rest of this book. So, if you want to skip the more serious crap, by all means proceed to chapter one.

At the writing of this book I was still doing the job, still putting in the hours and still playing dodgeball with some of my customers. I dealt with, like you, the public, every day, sometimes twenty, fifty, one hundred or more complete strangers. I had done this since I was ten years old. My social norm was developed with barriers between me and people; a desk, a sales counter, a waitress pad, a telephone, a grill line, a maid's cart, a cash register, a computer, a name tag. These things were the stage where sincere, albeit well-rehearsed scripts orchestrated my social interactions. A comedically-timed comment, inquisitive humorous banter to draw customers out and to form a tone of a relationship. Most of the time not a real one; as I may never see this person again— rather like a singer performing in falsetto.

I started my career as a naïve ten-year-old girl and by the time I graduated high school I had earned more than just my first piece of paper to hang on the wall. I had already put eight years of hard work under my belt: housekeeper, laundry person, front desk attendant, cook, dishwasher, waitress, bartender, cashier, pool person, landscaping construction, thrower, billing, and receptionist. It's funny how important that piece of paper on the wall becomes, regardless of your experience. I would chase paper my whole life like an exhilarated child running after the perfect snowflake just to have it dissolve on your tongue.

I was always the band geek, a nose-in-a-book, jeans and a t-shirt, no makeup, tree climbing kind of girl. Both of my sisters, one older, one younger, were beautiful, blonde, bright-eyed, intelligent cheerleaders who didn't leave the house without their faces on. My brother was the life of the party and smarter than he knew; a gifted smartass who could sell ice to Eskimos. He also had great hair. All my friends wanted to date him, and he knew how to talk to the ladies.

After a traumatic car accident in high school left me temporarily friendless and looking like a gag reflex-inducing freak for my freshman and sophomore years, I became an expert at anything but myself. I voraciously read books to hide from the world or escaped for hours practicing my flute, an instrument I took up at the age of eleven, endlessly repeating the notes on paper, searching for beauty and perfection through the melodies I played. I made an art out of chasing my parents' dreams instead of my own. Their chaos became mine and it took me nearly a lifetime to realize I deserved to chase my own dreams and to un-script my life.

In the midst of it all, I lived my life. I married Eric, my high school sweetheart and the love of my life. Together, we had three beautiful children: Our oldest was a boy, which scored points with my Hispanic in-laws, as a namesake had been born. (He was the first grandchild on both sides of the family.) Next came our adorable bouncing baby girl, which garnered me even more favor with the in-laws, as they had only had sons. Over the next few years Eric and I suffered more than one miscarriage and wondered if we were done. Eventually, we were blessed with our rainbow baby, a beautiful dark-haired baby girl. Our family was complete.

I gained immeasurable real-life experience in too many professions to count, and I chased paper for my walls, always looking for personal validation, self-worth or fulfillment. Some "wallpaper" was thrust on me through mandates manifested by my parent's ambitions and some was me searching for and repeating empty affirmations instead of seeking and finding my passions.

On the other hand, the flexibility in my increasingly

demanding job enabled me to go back to school while working more than fifty hours a week and taking care of my growing family. One of the perks of my work was that I could take my kids with me until they were about two years old. Granted, with each of them I worked up until the day of or day before I gave birth and went back to work two days after having each of them. Yep, answering phones and at my desk with a baby in my arms. (I would not recommend this, as it cost me dearly years later. A woman's body is not intended to have three kids, all weighing over eight pounds and overdue, and go back to work so soon.)

Right out of high school I headed, begrudgingly, to my one and only semester at Arizona State University and flunked because I was miserable being away from Eric and nothing else seemed to matter. While this was wonderfully romantic and it worked out in my long-term life plan, I couldn't shake the feeling that I had left my education undone. Even though I was damn good at my job, I wanted that piece of paper on the wall that said it.

Shortly after my first daughter was born, I enrolled at Eastern Arizona College..... and I loved it. Yes, I was one of those students everyone loves to hate; I would do every bit of extra credit even though I was already getting an A in the class. Nerds and geeks unite. While music and literature were my passions, I majored in business, as I had been conditioned to believe it would serve me well no matter where my life took me.

My one education goal, regardless of which degree, was to

graduate college before my kids graduated high school. Given my exacting work schedule and wanting some semblance of a personal life, this was a pretty lofty goal. At times I questioned my path, doubting it was ever going to happen. Often, I questioned whether I should spend the money and invest the time for the next semester.

I would remember that the callous, untroubled clock, would march on no matter what I did or didn't do. At the end of those three and a half months, I could either be one or two classes closer or not. It was up to me. My husband would nudge me with a hug and tell me he was proud of me, even for just one class. This sentiment was echoed by my parents and kids.

I achieved my goal. I graduated college with my bookkeeping certificate and AAS in business administration—just two weeks before my son graduated high school, my oldest daughter graduated junior high and our youngest graduated kindergarten. A banner year for the Mayhew's; a newfound confidence and another piece of paper—or two—for my wall.

Over the years my parents kept their classic and cozy little roadside diner and the mom-and-pop motel, while expanding their domain to include a tri-state waste management company in Arizona, New Mexico and Colorado. Through having my kids, I worked, more than full-time hours as the Office/Operations Manager for the garbage company. I was in charge of three landfills, six transfer stations and over six thousand residential, commercial and industrial customers spanning six counties in Arizona and New Mexico. I did everything from hiring and firing, governmental reports, training, contract negotiations, billing, to picking up windblown trash at the landfill sites.

As the western slope of Colorado offered a larger more diverse community and opportunities, it didn't take my parents long to purchase a home there. Soon my three siblings followed, all managing different aspects of the company there. For months at a time my parents would be in Colorado instead of Arizona. During these times, I was unapologetically chained to the mom-and-pop, unable to leave my parents' never-ending, ever-expanding 24/7/365 nightmare of responsibility.

"We can't spare the payroll" was the resounding chorus, to my request to having someone twenty-four hours a day at the mom and pop. So, I was voluntold for this delightful duty, with our growing little family in tow.

My mornings started early. At dawn I would unlock the front lobby door, assign hotel rooms to be cleaned and garbage routes, start a load of hotel laundry, and a load of our laundry, feed the kids, and check out guests. Then Eric or I would load our kids and drive the twelve miles to feed our dogs, check on our lonely little home and drop the kids off at school, or if it was the weekend, with my in-laws.

Work all day, pick up the kids, supervise homework, check in guests, make dinner, give showers, check in guests, go to my classes, tuck kids in bed, check in guests, do my homework, check in guests. Reprieve came when all the routes were done, trucks were parked, and guests were in. That is when I could lock the lobby door, give my kids a second silent kiss goodnight and snuggle in next to Eric with a prayer for my family and that the evil night door buzzer would not interrupt my dreams. This went on for a decade; two weeks home, six weeks motel, three weeks home, 5 weeks motel. It was the real-life, honest to goodness version of walking two snow-covered miles up the hill to school, both ways.

After my last child was born, I hit the ground running and went to work full-time in an all too familiar field: managing my parents' newly constructed, three story, Franchise Flagged hotel. I started just a few weeks before it opened, so there were endless tasks to accomplish. Computer systems had to go live, new linens needed to be washed and folded, beds needed to be made, rooms had to be staged, employees needed to be hired and trained. It was my first time actually opening and managing a gleaming, modern, newly branded Franchise Flagged hotel. I was excited.

I was also going to have to be certified as a general manager. I flew across the country to my first formal training in the hospitality business. It was surreal. I realized for the first time that I knew more than I thought, but I also learned why I did some of the things that I did and what the industry terms were for those things. I came away more confident in my abilities.

My parents continued to add to their empire—and my nightmare—with four hotels and two restaurants in Michigan, a miniature golf course, a theatre, two more hotels and a new convention center, gift shop and restaurant, so big, the old diner would've fit on just the outdoor patio, in Arizona. I was charged with managing everything in Arizona—no small task, given I had no experience in managing a theatre, miniature golf course, or gift shop.

I didn't believe in managing without knowledge, so I dutifully did what I had been taught to do.... rolled up my sleeves and jumped right in. As quickly as I could, I learned as much as I could. I learned how to load the movie reels, sell tickets, pop popcorn, and clean a theatre between shows. I learned how to operate the batting cages, how to sell golf clubs, and how to appeal to the schools. I learned how to sell larger convention space and how to buy for the gift shop. I learned three or four more computer systems, and I learned how to do flowers.

With the new hotels came new brands, different franchise flags, and more trainings. I was required to become a certified hotel administrator through an accredited industry-recognized program. It required a certain amount of experience, formal education, community involvement and continuing education. I completed what I needed to and earned another piece of paper for my wall.

Like this all wasn't enough, my husband and I eventually bought two hotels of our very own. I don't know what the hell I was thinking. I had been stuck on the fervent, ever-speeding merry-go-round of my parents' serial entrepreneurship for decades and now I was doing it to myself. I was frustrated and exhausted. The stress, both inconsequentially and sometimes unappreciatively, piled on by my parents' ambition and some self-inflicted, weighed on my soul and I ended up in not a very good place, physically or emotionally.

As I watched my children, husband and my siblings attain their goals outside of the drama-filled funny farm I worked in,

I realized I wanted that too, and they wanted it for me. They told me it was about time I listened to my own advice, that I had to live what I loved, whatever that was and however I could.

I wanted to put down the script, but I didn't know how. I was scared shitless. I had been safe inside that manuscript for decades. I had to tell my parents I was resigning, and I had to tell people who had become more than co-workers or team members that I was leaving. I felt like I was abandoning all of them and part of myself. I had to relinquish control of not only my job, but my life. I lamented over the decision for years, with the ideas and stories for this book filling notepads, scraps of paper, texts to myself and my dreams. Every hilariously fucked-up customer service situation I encountered made me think, *One day I'm going to write a book.*

Well, "One day" finally came. My amazing husband was set to retire, and I knew I had to do something, anything that fulfilled me, and I loved writing, telling my stories and making frustrated Service Warriors laugh. I had something to say, I had a life to live, I had a path to find. My husband and I sold our hotels, my letter of resignation was written, tears were shed, and sleep was lost. I gathered my notes, along with my courage, and I started to write; seriously write. The staying-up-till-three-in-the-morning-and-not-even-tired kind of writing. My husband told me that me not being tired meant I had found my passion. (Thank you, my love.)

Now you know who I am and more importantly why I am. Enjoy.

CHAPTER 1

100% Satisfaction Guaranteed
The Customer is Always Right
The Customer is King

(My Suite A$$!)

I researched all of the above sayings on our wonderful World Wide Web to see how this bullshit all got started and you know what I found? Nothing. Nada. Not a Damn Thing. You know why? Because I don't think anyone really has the balls to lay claim to being the dumb ass who would have originated such sugar-coated utterly stupid ideologies, mantras, phrases or terms. You want to know why I looked it up? Karma, that's why.

Yep, I was going to call, text, email, write a strongly worded letter, put up a massive billboard in Times Square or take out a full-page ad in *The New York Times*, calling anyone out who would like to own this and possibly sue them for all the pain, suffering and emotional turmoil it has caused, just in my life and jobs alone. I think it would be a valid case, don't you? Class action even. Hell, yeah you do—that is, unless you are one of those one percenters. Wouldn't you just like to smack that genius, shake them and yell in their face, "What were you thinking????????!!!!!!!!!"

I will probably repeat this a lot in writing this book: I believe in great customer service, I really do, and I believe in taking care of a problem when something goes wrong with whatever service or product you are supplying to a customer. I 100% believe if it is our fault or defective, then it is our duty and responsibility to our customers to do everything we can to make it right and to apologize.

We all know, though, that is not how that shit works all the time. It would work if we lived in a perfect fucking world, but we don't. It would work if everyone was fucking honest, but they aren't. It would work if these giant FUCKING corporations would back their shit up, but they won't.

Fair warning: In the introduction I alluded to the fact that I had done quite a stint as the office manager for a two-state garbage company. Well, I did that for over a decade, working primarily with men—more specifically, garbage men. I am not profiling or grouping them together, just saying that in our company the foul language flowed freely and, at times, mixed with a pretty raunchy sense of humor.

They were great guys with an extremely hot, dirty disgusting job, and they always tried to be respectful around me. However, I believe, hell, I know—that some of their vernacular rubbed off on me. I have tried over the years to rein in this habit and have been somewhat successful. It just seems to weave its way into my exasperated storytelling, especially when I'm on a roll.

You know who created these asinine catchphrases and hollow mantras, used to lure customers and keep them loyal? Big corporations, that's who. Good customer service is not rocket science. It always has been and still is fairly elementary. We all learned it in kindergarten: The Golden Rule. If you are, as I have described above, honest, hardworking and ethical, then there should be no need to ever put those jacked-up phrases on a wall or put together unrealistic guidelines to govern it by.

But no, I still remember the year I saw that happen. We had our first franchised hotel (I won't tell you which franchise, as I'm sure I would get in trouble for calling some pencil-pushing, keyboard-stroking, college-educated, no real-life experience committee, who didn't have to deal with customers face-to-face a bunch of dumbasses for doing it).

We received our first mandated plaque, one that said "100% Satisfaction Guaranteed" in 1997. By mandate, we had to put The Sign up on the wall right behind the front desk in plain and obvious site of all our valued guests, or we would be in danger of failing our inspection. That was all the plaque said. "100% Satisfaction Guaranteed", and in their corporate worldwide advertising, they screamed it from the rooftops, in television ads and in print: **"100% Satisfaction Guaranteed"** or your money back; or your first night free; or however any of these programs drew customers in and promised them the world. That sign would come to invoke the same skin-crawling feeling you get from hearing nails dragged down a chalkboard.

The FINE PRINT, however, was left up to us to explain to the actual customer, as it is always left up to the front-line customer service personnel to explain. Our FINE PRINT was: the guest couldn't just tell us at check-out, they had to have made us aware of the situation during their stay and given us the opportunity to fix it. Then it was at the discretion of the owner or general manager as to any compensation or refund.

Now come on, we all know this is how it works with loyalty programs: reimbursement promises, promotions or anything else big corporate decision-makers put out there for us, the grunts on the ground, to enforce and endure, while they hide behind their FINE PRINT, convenient hold button and mind-numbing elevator music.

I swear, somewhere there is some elusive secret university degree—in the legal field, of course, focused exclusively on FINE PRINT.....how to word it, when and how to make it known and available, and, of course, how to make sure that none of the little minions who develop the program or write the FINE PRINT will ever have to answer a phone call or talk to an actual customer about it. Jesus Christ, it is beyond frustrating and annoying.

I just want to tell those professional sugar-coating committee members to FUCK OFF! You know why? Because about three months into instituting programs like these, those executive slackers are having a party or dinner with plenty of booze, patting each other on the back and listening to customer service recorded conversations for entertainment. Laughing their asses off at their team's expense. And, from all my experience, they aren't using it to train anybody.

My use of front-line customer service or grunts on the ground phrasing is no accident. When you have a screaming, irate, irrational, privileged, dishonest customer in front of you or on the phone, you are in the trenches in a confrontation that someone brought to you. (No disrespect to our wonderful military and emergency service personnel, not even close to what you all do on a daily basis. Thank you for your service.)

It didn't take long for the jackasses and psychos to come out, after putting up The Sign. The first time I had to deal with this was a doozy. I was in my office doing what seemed like mundane paperwork, in retrospect, when my frazzled front desk clerk came and asked me, in an exasperated voice, if I could come and talk to an upset guest at the desk. She let me know that the guest didn't want to be charged for her stay the night before. She was demanding to talk to the general manager and wouldn't explain why. I asked what room it was, and the attendant told me. As the flustered front desk attendant retreated to tell the guest I would be right there, I quickly looked up the guest's info to see if I could glean any clue as to her dissatisfaction or if notes had been made in the front desk log during her stay. Nothing, absolutely nothing.

So, frustratingly ignorant, I steeled myself and went out front, greeted the guest by name and introduced and identified myself. I noticed she was a short, stout woman around fifty-five or sixty years of age and at least four hundred pounds. As I extended my hand for a friendly firm shake, she waved it away with one quick stroke of her puffy, stubby, well-manicured hand, and asked me if I was the general manager. Guessing she had missed the fact that that was how I had just identified myself, I replied yes and asked, with appropriate politeness, how I could be of assistance.

If contempt has a look, that is how she looked at me when she sarcastically asked, "Why aren't you wearing a name tag?" In my head I was sincerely hoping that a team member name tag infraction was not what had irritated our guest to this degree. Smiling, I gave her my well-practiced, tried and true, perfunctory response: "I like to interact with our guests without the restriction or influence of titles."

She, immediately, chastised me for being unprofessional and, with a mother's disdain, accentuated by a well-timed eye roll, simply told me she wasn't going to pay for the night before and pointed her chubby determined little index finger at The Sign. I asked her if there had been a problem during her stay, as I didn't see anything noted in her room notes or in the front desk logbook as having been reported.

It was on. She told me there was something wrong with the water in our pool. I must have looked perplexed because she rambled on. She didn't know what was wrong, but there was something amiss. Between huffs, puffs and the occasional sprinkling of spittle that hit my face, she managed to recount how she used the pool the night before and tried it again that morning and that there must be something terribly wrong with the water in our pool, because she didn't float right.

Long pause here as I took a confused moment to look around for the hidden camera and, at the same time, contemplate this entire scenario in my head. No shit, this four-hundred-pound, aging, spitting, female Floating Hobbit wanted her room for free because she didn't float right—and obviously that was somehow our fault, as she determinedly pointed out The Sign.

I bit the inside of my cheek, trying to suppress the urge to laugh, because that would just be unprofessional—absolutely warranted but unprofessional. I asked her to excuse me for just a moment. I walked around the corner and perused the footage from the security cameras, as maybe the water in the pool had mysteriously drained or magically turned to concrete, and no one had told me. No, the pool and hot tub were both full of actual water and crystal clear.

I walked back out and let the guest know there seemed to be nothing wrong with the pool and apologized if it was different than where she had floated in the past. Next came the rantings of the angry, bloated Floating Hobbit. My front desk team member and I were subjected to the exaggerated tales of all the places she had floated and for how many years she had been floating, and that the possibility of floating was the only reason she stayed at our hotel and that, because of our faulty water and completely inept staff, she had a miserable stay.

That chubby, wrinkled little finger came out again, this time more forcefully, pointing at and reciting The Sign, The Sign, The God Forsaken Ever Lovin' Sign. I again apologized for the inconvenience and told her there was nothing I could do at this time. Turning on her overly stressed kitten heels, and with a huff of dissatisfaction, she enlightened me with the tale of how she was going to ruin us with a well-deserved, in her own mind, call to corporate. In the same breath I was adamantly informed that I was just a bitch. With that, the angry, Little Floating Hobbit was gone.

Sure enough, less than twenty-four hours later I had a formal complaint from the franchise, who, of course, did nothing to back their shit up, only deferring it back to us with the threat of a one hundred and fifty dollar fine if not answered in a timely and approved manner.

In response to these types of incidents we were supposed to be able to contact our customer service support center or General Manager Coaching Line for assistance on how to handle difficult customers or situations. Trainings were offered at conventions, and mindless insincere form letters were written; all you had to do was add customer names.

When my front desk supervisor, Becki, and I were at our first convention following the compulsory hanging of The sign, we asked the trainer why, when a customer called them first, didn't they explain their FINE PRINT and inform the guest that they, the corporation—not us—had put those policies together. He responded by saying, "We just take down their information and/or complaint, we report it to you and give you forty-eight hours to close it to the satisfaction of the guest, or we fine you one hundred and fifty dollars."

My front desk supervisor and I thought, *hmmm, wait just a damn minute, let's try this again.* This time maybe with a hypothetical situation, as obviously this trainer must have misunderstood the question. Like a bullshit-spewing politician, he had expertly avoided answering our question and subsequently averted full eye contact.

With the stealth of customer service ninjas, we switched tactics and decided to try another method of attack. We laid out the hypothetical scene: A disgruntled customer calls a complaint into the customer service line and reports that their TV didn't work during their stay. "The complaint you sent to me says that the dissatisfied customer told you they did *not* tell anyone during their stay," I said to the trainer. "How come you don't stop it right then and there and let them know that they would have had to have notified someone during their stay? After all isn't that the hollow, empty, *fucking* worthless policy you people have put in place in your FINE PRINT?" (To my credit I did not use the F word with him, it stayed locked politely in my Ninja Service Warrior head.)

There they were. Those black, soulless eyes staring back at us like we had just asked a sixth grader to explain nuclear fission. He gathered himself for a moment, clearing his throat, adjusting his suit, and then said, "Well we want you to have that connection with your guest."

Oh damn, how much smoke can you blow up one person's ass, still not directly answer the question, deflect all responsibility back to me, and charge me one hundred and fifty dollars for the privilege of you doing it? Just shut the hell up!!!!!

I am beginning to think writing this is going to be therapeutic on some level.

The worst part of this story is that when we reviewed the security footage, the sweet Little Floater hadn't even used the damn pool. We ended up still giving her fifteen percent off her room just to keep the Lying Little Floating Hobbit happy. How many of you have done this? How difficult of a pill is this to swallow? How many of your bosses or your weak-ass company policies leave you feeling like a wuss, because you know you are right, you know the customer is lying and you are still required to smile, apologize and refund them?

All this to keep the numbers up, and those jackasses and lying psychos know it. It is hard enough to eat crow when you know you're wrong and need to apologize, and it is even more difficult to swallow your pride when it's questionable but worth it, but it is like trying to swallow an entire stick of butter when you know the person you are cowing down to is a belligerent, lying, scheming, little asshole.

The Floater was not the greatest of our 100% performers. Oddly enough, the one I most vividly remember was also a woman, roughly the same age, just a little lighter, and without the floating fetish. Her needs were of another nature. Her and her middle-aged, able-bodied "son" were from Vegas and had rented a lovely room with two queen beds and a balcony on the second floor.

The next morning, they were set to check out and we received a frantic phone call from her "son" in the room, saying that a large picture on the wall had fallen and hit his mother in the head and they needed an ambulance. My team called 911 while my head of maintenance, our breakfast attendant and I, who were all first aid trained, hurriedly headed to the room to offer what assistance we could.

We knocked on the door and the "son" quickly answered and let us in the room, the smell of obnoxiously applied perfume and cologne escaping past us. Anxiously, we entered the heavily scented room, ready to administer first aid if needed. Rounding the corner to the beds, we saw the elderly woman was still on the well slept in bed in her knee-length silky nightgown, with the large desert landscape picture still on top of her and moaning. Neither her nor her concerned "son" had taken the initiative to remove the heavy picture. Odd.

We removed the picture from the Silky Lady and set it aside. In doing so, my head of maintenance noticed the sheet rock screws, that securely held both the top and bottom of the picture into the wall, had been ripped right out and the picture had managed to jump the three-foot distance between the bed and the wall, accurately landing squarely on top of her.

I followed his gaze and, with a slight and knowing nod of his head, our questioning eyes met. We also noticed that older mother and dutiful "son" had only used one bed, as the other bed was untouched and still perfectly made, hence the word "son" in quotation marks. (Creepy, yeah, we see it all.)

Creepy Cougar wasn't bleeding and there were no bumps or contusions on her head or anywhere else. My breakfast attendant got a cold compress and offered it to her just in case. EMS arrived and assessed her condition, helping her gingerly sit up. They also could find no abrasions, bumps or contusions. They asked what medications she was on and the "son" pulled a gallon size baggie out of their luggage and held it up, making the sound of a maraca being shaken. The pill bottles were threatening to burst that poor piece of plastic at the seams. After taking her history and listing her meds, the EMTs offered to transport her to the hospital for observation. She refused their repeated urgings. The situation was now non-emergent and well in hand, so we excused ourselves and left.

On the way back down the elevator, my breakfast person let me know that both of those people had just been in for breakfast. I asked her if the woman had been in her nightgown or robe when she came down, and she said no, they both were fully dressed and, in fact, must have just went back to the room. The questioning maintenance man told me that there was no way that picture frame came out of the wall by itself and flew that distance.

I graciously thanked them both and assured them I would be taking care of the situation. As soon as I got back to the desk, I reviewed the security footage and, sure enough, both guests had just been down in the breakfast room fully dressed, not a silky nightgown in sight. The things that make you go *hmmmmmm!*

Well, it wasn't five minutes after the empty-handed dedicated ambulance personnel left when I heard a commotion at the front desk. The Creepy Cougar and her "son" or whatever he was, were loudly complaining at the black marble front desk that a picture had fallen on the woman and that they were going to sue us. They didn't want to be charged for their room, and they were loudly referring to The Sign. Predictably, they were deafeningly and most colorfully demanding to speak to the general manager. They were both being as rude and nasty to my befuddled front desk team member as they could be.

The hair was picking up on the back of my neck as I sat at my desk. My anger rose in the pit of my stomach and my hands started to shake as they always did when I reached my threshold for tolerance. I hated it. I hated it. I just hated it when I felt my anger so much that I either started crying or shaking. It made me even angrier, as I did not like allowing myself to be affected that way by the abundance of unreasonable assholes.

You could say almost anything to me or call me any name—and trust me, I had been called them all—and I would, for the most part, remain calm and professional. When you crossed that line and insulted, cussed at, yelled at, disrespected or threatened my team members, you had gone too far, and I would defend them with all that I had, just short of kicking your ass.

Immediately I came out from the back and asked if I could help, noticing that in that short amount of time (I swear only five minutes) the Creepy Cougar was fully dressed and miraculously recovered. The woman told me no, that she wanted to speak to the damn manager, not any more of us.

Remember when I said I never wore my name tag that identified me as general manager? Well, this was the perfect example of why I didn't. I got to see first-hand how my team members were truly treated by our valued, misguided guests and the privilege of being treated the same way, until I shut that shit down.

That is, unless we were getting inspected. Yes, I was fully aware of and appreciated the infinite list of jacked-up rules we all had to play by to satisfy the corporate world. Again, not always practical in the real world. That's why my name tag always sat safely and squarely in the same place on my desk. There needed to be some discretion allowed to protect our greatest asset of all: the team members that we wanted to, paid to, trained to and expected to take care of all our valued customers. Respect went two ways and I didn't care who you were or what the situation was, I expected it from and for my team, and nothing less

Well, at that, with my shaking hands resting on the cool black marble, I proudly and somewhat forcefully introduced myself to her as the general manager and you could audibly hear them both suck air. Suddenly her demeanor changed, as she now tried to portray this sweet old victim of a woman, throwing a seriously sickly moan to her voice and a weak-ass, now unsteady hand to her head. Her "son" instantly became disproportionately protective and doting, referring to The Sign and requesting, quite nicely and with a newfound, albeit too late, respect, that they not have to pay for their room.

Just as nicely and just as politely, I informed them that they knew I had been in their room, right after the incident. They were, more courteously than they deserved, informed that I had reviewed our security footage and seen them both fully dressed minutes before in the breakfast room and had noticed that when I went to the room, she was conveniently back in her nightgown. I told them how odd it was that no one had bothered to remove the heavy picture before we got there. As professionally as possible, I let them know that I didn't appreciate how they had been speaking to my team any more than I appreciated their performance.

I did apologize though. Hell, yes, I did. I apologized, quite sincerely, that it wasn't going to work this time. Now the next words probably should never have come out of my mouth. Maybe my bitch filter had been temporarily jammed by the con artistry of it all, and it just didn't reboot in time. Or maybe I just didn't give a shit at that point.

Either way, it was another apology, a very sweet heartfelt one at that. I apologized for something obviously being wrong with the other bed in their room as we noticed they had only used one and that must have been terribly unfortunate and uncomfortable for both mother and "son". Appropriately thwarted and embarrassed, they uneventfully left, heads down, and in a hurry. We never heard from the Creepy Cougar or her "son" again.

Sometimes I feel bad when I tell these stories. I don't want people to think I didn't appreciate my customers or didn't do all I could to make them happy. I absolutely did, we all did. I don't think there is any business owner out there that starts out their day wondering, "Hmm, what kind of an ass can I be today or how can I disappoint my customers the most?"

Okay I take that back. There is that one bar in Vegas where being an asshole server is the point and goal of your employment. That's their thing, and it is intended to be—and is—funny as hell. That would be the exception to the rule.

Our team was amazing and displayed great customer service, day in and day out. To make this point very real, let me tell you about one of our great customer service moments. You might at first think the guest was being a sexist ass, but it is all about perspective.

We had this very regular customer who stayed one night a week for one of the companies that served the local mine. He was the stereotypical Man's Man. You know, a hard-working, door-opening, "hello sweetie", laugh-at-his-own-jokes, male chauvinist. He was harmless, but still a male chauvinist.

Don't get me wrong, I love having a door opened for me, and in the hospitality business, the "sweetie", "sweetheart" or "honey" doesn't even register after a while. I only add this because God forbid, I offend someone, either the feminists or the men. Honestly, I think most guys who worked at the mine, were just too tired by the time they were checking in to read the name tag, and they meant no disrespect.

Every time this Man's Man checked in; he would politely be asked if there was anything else, we could do as we gave him the key to his room. A mundane question we asked all customers during the check-in process. Inevitably, he would always respond, "A blonde, you could get me a blonde." He would laugh heartily and walk away, confident that his sense of humor was appreciated.

We could have just chalked it up to borderline harassment, but I had a plan for his next visit. It addressed his response and just might stop him from putting it out there in the future. At least that's what I hoped for. I was raised knowing two things: 1) You can fight sarcasm with humor and 2) An asshole's money spends just as good as anyone else's.

I waited with anxious anticipation for his next incoming reservation, and soon enough, the glorious day arrived. I was well prepared. When Man's Man walked through the glass doors, I happily checked him in myself, gave him his keys and dutifully asked the innocent question. Sure, enough his rye little sexist response was exactly as it had always been. I just smiled a Cheshire Cat grin and told him to have a good evening, as he walked away laughing. My team members and I were damn near giddy with excitement, wondering if we would get a response to the fulfilling of his request.

When he opened the door to his room and trudged in his luggage, like he had done every week for the last year, there sat his blonde. Sitting proudly on his ergonomic work desk was a blonde doll, ready and willing to fulfill his every wish. She was accompanied by a hand-written note saying, "This is the best we could do. Your committed front desk team." He came down to the desk, laughing like hell. Sure enough, he never uttered those words again. Yep, there were no limits to what I wouldn't do to please a customer, as long as it was legal and moral. It's said if you can't beat them, join them.

My team and I both learned a valuable lesson that day and so did he. Sometimes, we just needed to think outside the box and not take everything quite so literally. Just like those 100% customers should not have taken The Sign literally and mistaken our hospitality and the imitation gold-framed sign for stupidity.

For the Man's Man, he could stay anytime. As for the Floater and the Creepy Cougar, they could both never return and go FUCK OFF!

The time wasted in therapy is endless.

CHAPTER 2

Suite Sex and Nudity

(Do we really have to explain this shit? Apparently, we do.)

Sex.
A touchy subject where I come from, as it is predominantly a very religious, conservative community. Sex isn't talked about, and God forbid...done, ultimately, until you are married. After that you can fuck like rabbits to repopulate the earth.

I don't necessarily agree with that but then again, I don't have to. I have always been thankful that my parents were a little more progressive and accepting of all people. They taught me everyone's sexuality is their own and what you do behind closed doors is just between you and whomever. If everyone was a consenting adult and comfortable, it was all good.

Key here is—in case you missed it—behind closed doors. Behind Closed Doors. I cannot stress that enough.......Behind Damn Closed Doors! If you think it is unnecessary to say it or explain it, you would be wrong.

First time this came into play for me I was just the curious tender age of twelve or thirteen, and completely inexperienced in this department. I hadn't even kissed a boy yet. One bright and blistering hot Sunday afternoon I was unexpectedly and thoroughly educated in this area when I was sweating my ass off cleaning rooms. To be fair, it was totally and completely my own fault.

At the old mom-and-pop, guests parked right in front of their cozy little casita rooms or in the shaded carports next to them. It would stand to reason if there was no car, it was safe to assume they had checked out. No car was parked at the next room on my cleaning list. Guest must be gone.

I put the key in the lock and proceeded to break the cardinal rule of any hotel employee.... always, Always, ALWAYS knock and announce before entering a room. No Exceptions! Nope, I just used the master key and opened the door and there it was—my first X-rated experience.

I was unexpectedly confronted with a completely nude honeymoon couple in the spooning position, her front to me and his hands over her boobs. Honestly, I think I stood there for a minute not sure what I was seeing, my eyes wide and mouth agape. They never even broke stride. Pretty impressive now that I think about it.

I slammed that door shut and moved that maids' cart, as

fast as my wobbly jelly legs would move, to the other side of the hotel. Linens were falling off; coffee cups and matches were flying as I frantically moved that cart over the gravel driveway, sweat stinging my eyes. I needed to be as far away as possible and collect myself. My entire body was shaking from embarrassment and my mind was racing, trying to process what I had just seen. This pornographic yet educational memory is still burned into my brain to this day.

Of course, on my way to the far opposite side of the motel is when I noticed their wedding car parked behind the motel. They had parked there so their friends wouldn't mess with the car. Not that that information did me any good now. I took my sweet, no longer innocent, time cleaning the next room and stayed in it until I knew they were gone. There was no way in hell I was chancing running into them.

No need for a birds and bees talk here. Don't get me wrong, Mom still had the talk with me, though it was, by then, completely unnecessary. I never told her what had happened until years later. Lesson here is always, always, always— while going at it in a hotel room, or hell even if you are just sleeping— throw the latch or use the deadbolt. Just in case. To this day I am never in a hotel room without the deadbolt fully engaged. I even test that shit just to make sure it works.

To the couple's credit, this one was, in all reality, behind closed doors and completely and utterly not their fault at all. It was all me. Or rather all them—and I do mean all of them— but it was no one's fault but my own. After that I wouldn't have cared if the Pope himself told me that someone had checked out. I would forever knock and announce, more than once, before going into any room. Period.

Oddly enough, the next experiences involved my amazingly handsome husband and our garbage crews. (Yes, in case you skipped over the *I* intro thing, I also did a nearly decades long stint as the manager of a garbage company.) The first experience was when my husband came in all exasperated and sweating to me at the desk, not sure of what to do. After he told me what was going on, I wasn't sure if he was sweating from the miserably hot Arizona sun or from the experience he had just had.

He was at the hotel graciously helping my parents out by digging up a sewer line. (That is just the kind of man he is. Someone needs help, he is there. whether you're torn apart in an accident or are a friend in need, my husband will be there.)

He was on my dad's well-worn blue Ford tractor and was working between the house/office and the pool, in plain sight of the full courtyard on the east side of the motel. He was intently working the controls when he noticed a woman open the door of her room across the parking lot. The movement caused him to glance up from his work and he said his first thought was, *Nice bikini*. Then he realized it wasn't a bikini at all, but rather nothing but a hand towel over her breasts, and nothing else.

Fur Bikini Babe sauntered out to her car, making eye contact with my husband, opened the rear car door and, with great exaggeration, dropped the towel. She then aimlessly and unhurriedly finished getting what she needed out of the car, never picking up the towel. Only then did she walk unabashedly, buck naked, back to her room.

My husband didn't know where to look or what to do; things like that just hadn't happened to him before. When she was finally back in her room, he jumped off that tractor in a single leap, like his ass was on fire, and came in and told me what was going on. A gentleman through and through.

I called the room, and Fur Bikini Babe's "brother" answered the phone and told me his sister had emotional issues and sometimes did things like that. He said it like it was no big deal, like she walked her happy, naked ass out in public every day. I informed him that regardless of his sister's emotional state, and especially if he was aware of it, he needed to make sure she was dressed appropriately before going out in public. Duh, did we really have to explain this shit to people? It appeared so.

Our garbage crew was involved in my next experience. A couple of the guys had come to pick up the garbage at the motel. We weren't surprised to see them come into the office, as they would often come in while they were there to see if there were any messages for their route, to use the restroom, or just to get something cool to drink.

This time was different, though. They were laughing and smacking each other like embarrassed schoolboys. We were all wondering so I asked, "What's going on?" They could hardly get it out: There were women sunbathing topless at the pool. Thinking back, I am more than a little surprised they came in and told us at all.

We quickly left our desks to look out the back window and sure enough, by God, there were two tall, beautiful, blonde, perfectly tanned (without tan lines) women comfortably lounging topless at our pool in modest, high and tight, sunny, rural Arizona. We turned away from the window to go see if we could figure out who the Bare-Breasted Beauties were. Yep, we had checked them in; they were from Sweden. Bare breasts may not cause much of a ruckus in more European parts of the world, but in the conservative, religious West, they cause quite a stir.

We were left trying to decide who was going to go tell the Bare-Breasted Beauties or Swedish Twins they needed to put their tops back on. Of course, all the guys were volunteering to sacrifice themselves for the job. Knowing better than that, my mom won out and made short work of schooling the Swedish Twins in American customs.

Key here: **Educate yourself on local customs, traditions and laws before you travel**. This shit will get you arrested or at the very least ogled at by strangers. I guess in this case we really did need to explain that shit.

Sometimes, though, it was the locals that did this crap or pissed you off—take your pick. One time, and one time only, we hosted a female stripper show in the convention center adjacent to the saloon. Yes, I said saloon; again: rural Arizona. I found out this was so not worth the aggravation nor the moral conflict. I ended up trying to explain to my daughters that no, I would not be okay with them doing that to pay for their college education.

After explaining that to them there was no way in hell, I could justify us making money from it ourselves, yet not condone it for them. I don't know about you, but I find it pretty damn difficult to talk out of both sides of my mouth.

Surprisingly, the men and women who put on the show were really nice people. Kind of creepy that they had their young kids help put their fliers out on the tables, but very nice. We had promised the local ladies, that if we brought the female strippers, we would, at another time, bring the men for a show as well. Same company did both, so we were tied into the contract. Not sure which scared me more—legal action or disappointing the frustrated females in town if I didn't bring them. The male show went great, a packed house, and I am here to tell you that what they say is true: Women make for a much raunchier audience for this type of thing than any men I know.

One of the overly tanned well-muscled male entertainers was genuinely concerned that we would have security at the hotel, as in the past they had had issues with women following them to their rooms uninvited. They didn't appreciate it when it happened. I thought, how noble. We got this! By the end of their show we made sure we had plenty of security at the hotel to assure that the strapping well-built strong men got to their rooms safe and sound. Oddly enough, the female strippers had not requested or required this same service.

After escorting the Ripped Strippers to their rooms, they asked if we could open the indoor pool, after hours so they could relax, swim and maybe take in a sauna. As has happened so many times, we obliged only to have it come bite us in the ass later. Wanting to make sure the property and guests were secure; we were still at the property about an hour after the show just to ascertain all was quiet and that it stayed that way.

Everything seemed to be buttoned up and I was just about to leave when I glanced at the security monitor, on my way out, and saw odd flashes of movement in the pool area. Who feels the need to take that last glance at the security screen? My dumb ass, that's who. I went to investigate. Damn, damn, damn, I just needed to quit doing that shit.

I opened the door and was hit with the steamy acrid smell of chlorine and sex. One Ripped Stripper and a girl were swimming happy as can be, naked in the pool, and another was vigorously banging a moaning girl from behind, while she was laying over the edge of our hot tub, swinging her long black hair from side to side with every moan. Both naked as a jay bird. My knee jerk gut reaction was an incredulous "What the hell?"

At the sound of my exclamation, everyone suddenly grew modest and all parties dropped below the water line. I was pissed as hell and tried desperately (and failed) to keep some shred of professional composure when I told them, "How dare you disrespect this place. Go do that shit in your rooms!"

Keep in mind the very large indoor pool room was well lit and surrounded, on all sides, by windows that faced the main highway through town. I mean literally, it was less than one hundred feet from the road.

The two, in the pool, started getting out and gathering their things, but the Naked and Banging Girl in the hot tub was now gratuitously incensed and suddenly proper and prudent. She wanted to know if I was going to turn around while she got out of the hot tub. I spat back, as I nearly broke off the pool room door handle, "Really? You're concerned about being seen now? I guess you didn't notice the other two people in the room, the walls of glass windows or the two security cameras in the corners. I don't know what the hell y'all are doing tomorrow but I'm selling this shit on the Internet!"

Lord I was mad, and what made it worse is that I recognized Naked and Banging Girl. She was an administrative secretary we worked with on a regular basis who routinely booked hotel and meeting rooms for subcontractors that fed the mine. *God, I screamed in my own head, how am I supposed to work with her now that I have seen her naked and banging?*

I was adding up in my head all the money in sales that my inability to filter was going to cost me. And you know what? Wasn't as hard as I thought it would be. When we did see each other again, Naked and Banging acted like nothing had ever happened. Always shocked the hell out of me. So much for noble strippers and innocent locals.

One of the most entertaining ones, though, involved cowboys—naked cowboys, to be more specific. Stop thinking what you're thinking. No, we did not bring back the strippers. Told you we never would, and we never did. In this case, didn't need to. This time there was music and naked cowboys, free of charge. Didn't cost anyone anything but their self-respect.

A beautiful couple had a wonderful western wedding in the

reception hall for about two hundred of their closest family and friends. It was a memorable and joyous affair. The evening was winding down and people were starting to trickle out of the event and head to their hotel rooms across the road. Mostly the older folks taking the kids to tuck them in, to dream of princess brides and handsome grooms.

The wedding party and young adults were boisterously drinking, dancing and still having a good time. Some guests were on the dance floor and others were on the outdoor patio, relaxing and visiting. Old stories were being reminisced and new memories were being made by all. Love was in the air.

Foolishly, I was talking to and laughing with my team, prematurely chalking the evening up to another beautiful wedding, when my cell phone went off. A sound I had come to hate depending on the time, day and circumstance. It was the hotel. They had a problem with people in the outdoor hot tub. Honest to God, that is all they told me. I do not know why people consistently insist on leaving out important details. If they had been a little more accurate or forthcoming with some information, I would have been better prepared when I got there, and I probably would have brought at least one other person with me.

Walking across the street, I was foolishly thinking maybe some teenagers had jumped the fence for some fun. Again, I was wrong. The fence around the outdoor hot tub was an eight-foot tall, iron fence, and we locked the gate at ten p.m., so it was tricky getting in and even more so getting out. We had instituted certain measures to help discourage late-night fence jumpers.

I rounded the corner of the casitas, where the outdoor patio and gazebo-framed hot tub were and discovered three very naked cowboys proudly lounging in the hot bubbly water, wearing nothing but cowboy hats and a smile. Their clothes were outside the eight-foot metal rail fence and I saw that they had used the pool furniture that was outside the fence to climb over. While the Cocky Cowboys had lost their clothes on the way, they all managed to hang onto their beers.

Their wives were all casually sitting outside the fence in the patio area and were no help at all. They just looked at me like, "Your problem not ours." Wives and Cocky Cowboys were all laughing and having a great time, oblivious to the goings-on around them. And here I was, Miss Mildly Amused Killjoy. I told the cowboys to get out, get dressed and get to their rooms. I pointed out that families and children were walking back to their rooms for the night. To my amazement they agreed on the first request. They got out of the water to oblige, but soon discovered.... Houston, we have a problem. It never ceases to amaze me how quickly a person can sober up when you see the "Oh shit" look come across their face.

There was no pool furniture inside the fence, and they had nothing to help them climb back over...but each other. I told you we had instituted a plan. Do you think I was going to go and unlock that gate? Hell no! I might have, if anyone had thought to ask me, but they were all too drunk.

So, I watched with amusement as three naked cowboys awkwardly hoisted each other's bare, wet asses over that fence.

I would have been more amused if the Cocky Cowboys had looked more like our Ripped Strippers, but sadly that was not the case, especially after the cool Arizona night air hit their hot wet skin. It was all I could do to hold back my laughter.

Their wives were laughing like hell while I busied myself trying to block the view from passing guests. They finally accomplished their task and landed on the other side of the fence, again never losing their beers. Was this wrong? Yes! Was it funny? Hell, yes it was funny! After successfully scaling the fence and not snagging balls, dropping beers or anything, they started getting dressed and I left, naively thinking that would be the last I would see of them. Hah! Wrong again.

I went back to check on the wedding and, before I knew it, the Cocky Cowboys and their wives were standing at the patio gate wanting to come back in and rejoin the reception. The blissfully unaware mother of the bride summoned me and asked if it would be okay if they came in. I declined.

She tried to convince me by assuring me that I just didn't know cowboys, that they were simply blowing off some steam. Not to be outdone, I let her know that I had been married to a cowboy/cop for fifteen years and the last time he was naked in public, he was three. All she heard was cop and now, full of falsely placed hope, promptly wanted to take advantage of some non-existent brotherhood and told me that one of the cowboys was a New Mexico highway patrolman.

Damn! That did not make it better. In my mind I was screaming, *Why the fuck would you tell me that? Why the hell would you point him out?* In that case someone really needed to take their wet, drunk, dumb asses home and put them to bed.

The Cocky Cowboys were safely escorted, fully clothed and dry, back to their rooms and tucked in for the night. The party went on and ended beautifully without any further incidents of nudity. I never told the bride, but I always wondered if someone else did.

For shits and giggles, when I got home, I woke up my cowboy/cop husband and told him what happened. I asked him how drunk he would have to be to let one or two of his buddies hoist his naked wet ass over an eight-foot iron fence. My husband is six foot one, and kind of contemplative when he speaks. Even in his sleepy state he looked at me with the straightest face and without missing a lick, said, "There isn't enough beer in this whole county."

If you know that you do dumb shit when you drink, especially naked dumb shit, then you might think of following one, or better yet all, of these simple dumb drunk ass rules:

- Do not drink
- Only drink in a town where no one knows your dumb ass
- Only drink with family or friends who are sober enough or love you enough to stop your dumb ass
- Leave all devices with the ability to record in your car, so no one can record your dumb ass
- If someone does record you, make sure your dumb ass gets paid for that shit
- If you know you are a naked drunk, dress for it, zippers or buttons up the back Hell, put a lock on that shit

There are a lot of things that need explaining in this life—where babies come from, how to apply for a job, why folks die—but when and where it is appropriate to have sex or get naked should not be one of them. Hint, if you are in public, keep your damn clothes on; a swimsuit, pasties, wet t-shirt, grass skirt, kilt, coconuts, something; even a strategically placed cowboy hat.

I would like to think that all inappropriate behavior could be blamed on alcohol, but that would be unfair to the liquor industry. At least with it, there would be a reason other than a complete lack of modesty and human decency. Some days you had to be more vigilant about who you were renting rooms to than others. These wary instances were during proms, graduations and really any occasion or celebration involving high school or college students. We had a strict rule, and that was that we did not rent to people under the age of eighteen.

While my parents were more open-minded than most in our community, they had hard and fast rules. My dad, the father of three girls, always said no one's teenage daughter was going to get pregnant in his hotel. After all he would say, "You can't be almost pregnant." This, of course, coincided beautifully with my mother's witty but no-nonsense advice to us girls about boys, which was, "Remember you can't stop Niagara Falls with a teacup." You really don't appreciate these words of wisdom and whimsy until you have kids of your own and fear drugs, sex and alcohol more than life itself.

When it came time for these special occasions, we were always hypervigilant at the desk. No minors, no one in formals, no one without ID, and local addresses or customers that paid cash for a room were always suspicious and duly warned. Nine times out of ten we would stop or catch the exuberant underage party goers. Horny, hormone raging young people could be very creative when they wanted to have sex in a real bed instead of the bed of a pickup truck. What's surprising though was the number of stupid-ass adults that were willing to help them.

Parents, older friends, aunts, uncles, older siblings, all more than happy to lend a helping hand. They would come in, rent a room and give the keys to their respective Precious Angels as gifts. Can someone say, "Here, please go out and make me a grandparent while your ass is still in high school"?

To their credit, some of these normally intelligent adults would do this completely devoid of suspicion regarding their sweet, innocent, trustworthy. responsible God-fearing teenagers. Sucked into the story of "My girlfriends and I just want to have a sleepover after prom, and wouldn't it be fun to have a slumber party at a hotel for my birthday, so we can swim and stay up all night and we won't disturb you and your household after a hard day's work?" I am sure here is where they would interject a well-timed innocent smile and pleading look.

Exactly how stupid or naive are people? I am here to tell you pretty damn naive and impressively, insanely stupid. If we even suspected that a party might be in the works or keys may be gifted, we duly warned whoever was renting the room. We would, in no uncertain terms, tell them if we found out they were partying or they were not the ones in the room, we would throw whomever out and not refund their money.

They would, of course, assure us they would never do anything like that. Alrighty then, keys would be slid across the cool black marble counter with a whisper of "Consider yourself properly warned."

Without fail, we would start seeing the telltale signs of trouble underfoot: Lots of activity in and out of a certain room or an inordinate number of phone calls to or from (this was pre-cell phone). There might be twenty teenagers walking through with backpacks or beach towels, or giggling couples in tuxes and formals.

These were the blaringly obvious signs. More skillful ones would be a rock seen, on the security cameras, wedged in a self-locking exterior door to hold it open. This way kids didn't have to go by the front desk and didn't need a key to open the side doors. One of my favorites—now, not then—was when the bowling alley behind us called to let us know that kids were scaling the balconies of the hotel up to the third floor and were hauling ice chests up with ropes.

Now, there was a subtle art to catching these parties and virginity-losing events at just the right moment. If you disturbed them too soon, everything was innocent enough and you're just the hard-ass old bitch that didn't trust young people. Who, of course, were infinitely more mature and intelligent than we were at their age.

Like a good stakeout, we would wait and watch. We would sit there with our feet up, anxiously waiting and intently scanning the security screens, chomping on apples from the breakfast room and sipping on forty-four-ounce sodas from the corner store.

We waited till it seemed that a reasonable number of people had arrived. You know, enough to get the party started but not enough to do any real damage. They would all just be getting smugly comfortable, feeling like they had gotten away with it. Little did they know, plans had been made, master keys were in hand, and karma was walking down the hallway to their room.

We would approach the door. Music was blaring, banging out a steady rhythm on the door to the room. We heard the "I am so grown up" laughter of teenagers who were sure they had pulled the wool over the eyes of the hard ass old bitch at the desk.

We stopped and waited a moment, and then knocked... lightly at first. (Because it's just fun.) Music suddenly was turned down to a reasonable level and we heard the jockeying back and forth of "Did you hear that?" We waited a moment, and after a minute or two the music, confidently, got turned back up.

We knocked again, this time louder, harder and announced, "Front Desk." Music stopped, and we would hear the frantic movement of young people trying to hide or get dressed. They had nowhere to go and because they were still expecting more people, or truly believed they had achieved clear sailing, the deadbolt had not been engaged. Lucky us. We opened the door to a game of freeze or red-light green light. Everyone would be staring back at us like a deer in headlights.

Sometimes it was just a sweet young couple hoping for a romantic evening. More often than not, it was a room full of teenagers—five, ten, twenty, or even more—and someone had managed to get ahold of alcohol. We would tell them, respectfully and in no uncertain terms, they had to get out. They would tell us, with unwarranted confidence, that so-and-so, their relative or whoever, had rented the room and we couldn't throw them out. Well then, I would offer my sincere apologies as I backed out of the room and would tell them, "By all means, continue."—not!

In response to that, I'd either call the number for the unfortunate person who had rented the room for their Precious Angel, or the police. Either way everyone was going home safely to sleep soundly in their own beds. Occasionally we would get confronted by the loving, caring, void-of-an-intelligent thought adult that had really rented the room.

They either wanted their money refunded and I was just a bitch that had forgotten what it was like to be young, or they were absolutely flabbergasted that their Precious Angel was hosting a balls to the wall party. The first one I could care less about as yes, I was young once, but you know what? I had the decency to party and/or have sex in the boonies, like everyone else.

I always kind of felt bad for the second type, as they really couldn't believe it and their motivations were well intentioned. Misplaced, dumb-as-fuck stupid, but well intentioned. What is it they say? The road to hell is paved with good intentions. Well, so is the path to unwanted teen pregnancy and date rape.

I had a well-planned and too many a time practiced speech for these ones.

I would sympathize with them from the get-go, letting them know that we realized they had the best of intentions and that we truly believed so did their Precious Angel. I likened it to the adolescent telephone game. It started out with just four of their dearest friends and then this friend would tell that friend and it would just snowball, through no fault of their own, and before you knew it they were caught up in a growing situation that they were just not socially equipped, at this innocent, precious age, to handle. Damn I was good!

This always worked. It put us and the dumbass adult on the same side and let them know that we did not blame them or their Precious Angel. Really, we wanted to tell them what a complete dip shit sucker they were, but hey, in this position, Precious Angel was going home safely and so was everyone else. Just punishments and lectures would be doled out and well deserved. Who was I to rub it in?

Remember the third-floor climbers and the ice chests being hauled up with ropes? Well I remember that one too. In fact, I will never forget it. Just sticks in my head like I inhaled a fucking goat head. (Sorry, you may have to be from the West to understand that analogy.) My husband and I had stopped by on our randomly rare date night so I could check on some paperwork, and were still there when the call came in. I couldn't just leave it for the poor front desk attendant to handle alone. After all, if that was truly happening, we had some impressively stupid, innovative and creatively courageous idiots on our hands who didn't mind risking their lives for a party.

In all honesty we didn't bust this one ourselves. Rather, we were handed it on a silver platter when that phone rang, and it was the owner of the bowling alley behind the hotel, politely informing us that people were scaling our hotel to the third floor, like cockroaches, and hauling what looked like ice chests up with ropes. The hell you say.

I admit it was kind of shocking to have someone tell you that people were climbing your hotel like superheroes on a mission. Given they were ascending all the way to a third-floor balcony on the north side of the building, it narrowed down the rooms it could be. I pulled up the list of the in-house guests in our system and only one of our balcony rooms on that floor and on that side was occupied. Wouldn't you know, it was a local address. The front desk attendant said it was rented by a forty-something woman for herself and her niece.

We reviewed the cameras and we didn't see anything through any of the regular entrances and our video cameras didn't cover the newfound adolescent jungle gym area that we needed to look at. I headed upstairs, master keys in hand, telling my husband I would call if I needed him. This time I didn't even want to knock on the door, for fear that one of the kids might try to leave the same way they came and get hurt in the process.

The rhythmic thump of the music met me as soon as I got off the elevator and sure enough, I was headed in the right direction. The music was getting louder the closer I got. A light knock and I used the master key to enter the room, announcing myself as I opened the door. I was greeted with at least twenty wide-eyed, scurrying teenagers, food, birthday cake, beer and booze. There was one lone female adult sitting, cross-legged, on the bed, the host of her niece's sixteenth birthday party.

Politely, I asked the kids to leave the room and sit in the hallway. No one moved. I asked again, this time more forcefully, and still muted silence, except for the sound of kids throwing liquor bottles off the balcony to get rid of the evidence. I called the police. With that, everyone's mouth miraculously came to life, grew a tongue, and they all had something to say.

My now aggravated plain clothes off-duty husband showed up first, because he was just downstairs, waiting for quality time with his wife. Because he was out of uniform, the kids and their freshly grown mouths and attitudes did not believe that my husband was an officer. It would have been to their advantage to have grown a brain along with the mouth and attitude they had been able to manifest in a split second. That is, until the wallet badge came out and his buddies in blue—or in his case brown—showed up and seated the now not so mouthy teenagers, along with their host, in the hallway outside the room.

You know one thing my husband hated was the spokesperson in groups like this. The ones that said they could have an underage boonie party because they were having it on private property. Well in that case, just go ahead and murder, beat, rape and steal, just do it on your own property and you'll be just fine. Idiot.

Well this was the case that night too. There was food, music, beer and booze, and no one except Old Enough to Know Better Aunty was old enough to drink, let alone buy. The officers asked all the little squatters where they got the booze.

Before they could even offer a half-hearted excuse or answer, the party girls' grown-ass adult Aunt raised her hand and smugly said, "It's mine, officers." Like it cleansed the room of all nefarious actions and behavior. Well, thank you for making the investigation a hell of a lot easier and, at the same time, proving just how absolutely, unequivocally, remarkably stupid you are. The officers had Old Enough to Know Better take a seat in the hallway alongside her niece and ungrateful grumbling guests and told her to relax while they wrote her twenty citations for providing alcohol to minors. It was going to take a while.

You would think that was the worst thing, but it wasn't. As the officers busied themselves, administering breathalyzer tests, writing citations and calling parents, Old Enough to Know Better started pleading her case. She was employed as a security guard for the local mine, they weren't hurting anybody, she could lose her job, she needed her job, blah blah blah. Lord, I can't set the font on this computer big enough or bold enough to adequately emphasize the word DUMBASS here.

What the hell is wrong with you? was just whirling around in my head. *One of those kids could have broken their damn neck!* was resounding even louder. And for what? An anything but sweet sixteen party, you idiot. All I can say is I'm glad I'm not a cop, judge, or lawyer, and don't constantly have to listen to this type of bullshit every single day. Now and then is bad enough. Old Enough to Know Better was subsequently convicted and did lose her job. Happy fucking birthday to you!

Occasionally one would completely get by me, and when it did, it just chapped my ass. I distinctly remember one that got past me. I never would've known it if the housekeeper hadn't called the front desk and demanded that I come to the room she was in. That's not true, it wouldn't have happened if the guest hadn't been a disgusting perv. Dutifully I reported to the room, knowing full well this was not going to have a fairytale ending, unless that story was out of Brothers Grimm. Only once was I ever called to a room to see how clean it was.

Sure enough, when I walked in, there were pizza boxes, food containers, soda cans, beer cans, and cigarette butts. The room was heavy with the smell of old food and stale smoke. It was a mess, with trash everywhere and pizza and chips ground into the carpet. The worst part of it, though, were the two used condoms stuck to the wall. My self-respecting housekeeper was refusing to peel them off, and rightfully so. As karma would have it, she nor I would need to.

This happened to be when all the rooms were still single-story casitas with exterior doors. Lo and behold, and lucky for us, we heard a car pull up in front of the room we were in. A cocky, barely old enough to shave young man nonchalantly sauntered through the open door and said he was there to get his girlfriend's sweatpants. Talk about bad timing.

Condom Kid got a lecture from two disgusted women who were old enough to be his mother, standing in front of his wall of condoms. I asked him if he thought it was okay to leave a room like this. He told me he hadn't been alone; that it was him, his girlfriend and another couple; that they had come to have a good time after prom. Like it made it better that he was not the only guilty party.

I told Condom Kid we could clean up the mess but that he needed to take care of detaching the condoms from the wall and disposing of them. In his defense, he promptly told me that only one was his. God dammit, I didn't need to hear that. It was bad enough one, now two, had gotten by us, but really, he just admitted that they all had sex in front of each other and I guess played a twisted version of pin the tail on the donkey with their used condoms. They didn't learn that game in Sunday School.

I told him I didn't give a damn whose condoms they were, he was going to clean it up, or the next phone call I made would be to his parents. With this, we handed him a garbage bag, a cleaning rag and the spray bottle. Disinfectant cleaning spray, of course, along with the best pissed off, guilt- and shame-inducing mother looks we had. We both stood there with our arms crossed and watched indignantly as Condom Kid cleaned up his mess and promptly departed, sweatpants in hand, but not his dignity.

Just a little side note here, as this has happened on more than one occasion to rookie housekeeping team members and maintenance crews alike. Mattresses nowadays are no turn mattresses, thank the Lord above. But back in the day, you rotated and or flipped mattresses every three months. This necessary task always proved to be an unwanted lesson in human sexuality. Magazines, cock rings, dildos—you name it, we found it. Do you have any idea how gross this is for us to find? It never failed; first timers would insist on being bare-handed when doing this, and to us veterans, it always proved to be one of the greatest self-correcting behavior scenarios. Rookies inevitably gloved up before the next bed.

People, please take your nasty sex shit with you. I say nasty, not because toys aren't fun, but because no one wants to know about, let alone touch someone else's. We will not put it in lost and found for you to reclaim at a later date. Gosh honey, did you remember to pack the giant vibrating dildo we used last night? I mean what? Did you honestly just forget to pack that shit? Doubt It!

I have a theory about this type of scenario. I figure you flew here, did not want that specific personal item found in a bag search or x-ray machine at the airport, so you left your toys at home and bought new ones after you touched down, and then would leave them for the same reason you didn't pack them. Throwing them away in the room also wasn't a viable option, because if ever confronted, you would not have the defense of, "It must have belonged to the previous guest." Brilliant, just brilliant!

I am here to say, for the sake of all housekeepers, room attendants, and maintenance crews everywhere: Please grow the hell up, own your sexuality and be proud of it. please do not leave it for us to find!

CHAPTER 3

ANIMALS

(IF THEY COULD VOUCH FOR THEIR OWNERS, THEY COULD STAY.)

O ur entire family loves animals, and we have always had pets or raised animals...dogs, cats, horses, cows, hamsters, goldfish, you name it. I make no apologies for not being a vegetarian. Nope, we eat meat and we like it. My husband, friends and family do hunt and have fun doing it. We truly enjoy eating wild game as much as looking at it in all its natural beauty. I won't call you an undernourished vegan if you don't call me a heartless animal killer. Fair enough.

Our pets are members of our family and we have had some amazing, intelligent animals. We love them dearly, but we do not travel with our pets, unless you count transporting them in a stock trailer or taking them for a day trip to the river or vet.

All hotels, resorts or motels fall into one of two categories: either they are pet-friendly, or they aren't. This means either they accept pets—usually for a nightly fee of at least $10/day and they may have dog runs and provide cute little plastic bags, so you can pick up your dog's shit with your near bare-naked hands—or they don't. To avoid these fees guests routinely sneak in their furry family members. Now if getting cheated out of ten dollars was the worst part of this story you wouldn't be reading this chapter and I damn sure wouldn't be writing it.

Many people love their fur babies so much they take them with them wherever they go and maybe take the fur baby love a little too far. We all know them: they carry miniature dogs in designer purses and put booties on animals that have managed to have successfully walked this earth for thousands of years without them. You ever wonder who cleans out that purse when Fi Fi shits in it? I have, and just may ask someone next time I see that.

For some reason these folks—whether it's a Yorkie or a pit bull, a bearded dragon or a hamster—expect everyone else to love their fur baby as much as they do. Rarely is this the case. (And my apologies, as technically, a bearded dragon does not have fur.)

When I was still in high school, I remember one of our only two housekeepers storming into the laundry room where my mom and I were busily folding sheets (yes you can fold a fitted sheet neatly, especially after folding thousands of them) and adamantly stating that she was not going into this particular room one more time. The guest was a young, introvert geologist working up at one of the mines, and he had been staying with us for the past six weeks. He was not scheduled to check out for another month.

My parents had recently bought the little coffee shop across the street, so we weren't the ones cleaning the rooms as much anymore, because we were all busy slinging coffee, flipping burgers and cleaning tables, so we asked why. With hands on her hips, she firmly said, "Come with me." With that, she turned on her heal and stomped out the door. We grabbed our keys and followed her to his room.

Our fact-finding mission was abruptly halted as we went to step onto the porch outside his room. Coiled up in front of his door was a rattlesnake. Yes, when you approach a rattlesnake there is that unmistakable, rack-you-to-your-core sound. We all stopped short in anticipation of that sound, our hearts racing, and our arms outstretched protectively in front of each other, as if we could save one another from sharp venomous fangs to our calves.

The sound never came. Silence. After what seemed like an eternity, Mom picked up a stick and poked the snake. It was dead. Now, that fanged demon of a decoy hadn't just conveniently died in that position, which meant that Ruthless Rock Man purposely coiled it up outside that door for pure shock value. Anywhere in the west, that is not funny.

Kicking that poisonous prank aside, we opened the door

and walked into the dimly lit room. The open door now illuminated the venomous menagerie, collected by Ruthless Rock Man. Inside we found primitively built individual boxes with crudely cut flimsy metal mesh for lids. These barely-there boxes were home to his cold-blooded collection of scorpions, a tarantula, a Gila Monster, a couple more rattlesnakes and even a rhinoceros beetle.

Holy crap, an exterminator's nightmare. But of course, a housekeeper's wet dream. We didn't explore, we didn't linger to investigate further, we just turned around and shut the door behind us as we left. My mom hugged the housekeeper and let her know that we would take care of it and thanked her for letting us know what was going on.

By the time Ruthless Rock Man got off work, we had his folio ready and he was politely informed that we had extended the courtesy of checking him out early and he was free to find more suitable accommodations for himself and his loosely contained collection of "pets." It was said with a smile, even though we really wanted to tell him what a twisted fuck he was for purposely trying to scare people. He went on his merry way either completely unconcerned with or genuinely ignorant of his behavior. We pitied our competition.

For those of you not familiar with Arizona weather, we have some dauntingly impressive storms called monsoons. They roll in midsummer through the fall, and come on suddenly and fiercely, with imposing thunder, unrivaled lightning shows, brutal winds and torrential rains. They come hard, fast and loud, and leave just as suddenly as they appear. Animals are instinctively aware of two things: peoples' characters and weather. Good ones react and warn us accordingly. These would be great qualities if this massive storm had not been combined with a pit bull who accidentally locked himself in a hotel room bathroom when the storm hit.

The head housekeeper came to me one afternoon and let me know that the room attendants couldn't get into a room on the first floor because there was a large dog loose in the room and he was aggressively barking when they tried to open the door. Setting my glasses and work aside with the cliché thought of "never a dull moment", I thought there was no better way to assess the situation than going to see for myself. After all, I had always been pretty good with animals. So off I went.

Nope, not this time. I didn't even get to open the door an inch when the unkenneled pit bull charged the door and started viciously barking and growling. I snapped that door shut, realizing I was not the dog whisperer I thought I was. Promptly I retreated to the front desk and tried contacting the number we had on file for the guest. No answer. The housekeepers were instructed to leave the room for the next day and I would talk to Doggy Daddy when he came back in.

Within an hour, a huge monsoon rolled in, and it was an epic storm. One of those where we'd lose power and would be frantically mopping the floor, trying to keep up with the water as it blew in through the front doors. While waiting for Doggy Daddy to return to his room, we checked in another guest a couple rooms down from the Perturbed Pit. This guest called about ten minutes after checking in and said there was a dog somewhere and it wouldn't stop barking.

Checking on the dog again, I discovered I could now open the door and get in the room. Scared by the storm, the dog had run into the bathroom, and now couldn't get out. He had accidentally closed the door behind him, essentially locking himself in the bathroom, and was now barking out of fear and frustration. For the second time that day, I found myself shutting the door and once again retreating to the desk, still trying desperately to get a hold of Doggy Daddy. No answer. We moved the new guest to a different room and waited.

Three hours later, Doggy Daddy finally showed up and I let him know what was going on and informed him that we needed to get in his room. He was gracious and responded with a confident, "No problem." On our way to the room, he entertained me with endless tales of how great his dog was, never any problems, never bit anyone, never barked, never, never, never.

He opened the door to his room and, sure enough, the dog was still in the bathroom—or, after opening the door to the bathroom, what was left of it. That damn dog had eaten an eighteen-inch hole through the wall in the bathroom almost out the other side. He had ripped the now-mangled metal frame away from the door and scratched the shit out of the door itself. You wouldn't have thought he was capable of such damage in just three hours, because now he was all kisses and wagging tails when Doggy Daddy opened the door. Pissed would be an understatement.

I let Doggy Daddy know I would figure out what the damages were and that the dog could not stay during the rest of his time with us. He would have to make some other arrangements for his beloved fur baby. Doggy Daddy tried to convince me that he would be okay, and that he was really a good dog. In my mind I thought, *You are unquestionably, undeniably, completely and utterly right. He is a good dog; you though, are an idiotic, irresponsible pet owner. The dog should have been in a kennel while you were gone.* Instead I smiled and stood by my decision. The next day we informed him we had charged eight hundred dollars' worth of damages to his credit card. Now it was his turn to be pissed.

He didn't think we should have charged him that much, since we were already charging him twenty dollars per day for the pet. I calmly explained to him that the pet fee covered the additional deep cleaning of the room after pets and their owners leave, which includes shampooing the sofas and the floors to prepare the room for the next guest—not for reconstruction and a new door and frame.

No matter the logic, Doggy Daddy was still pissed and took the position that we were just screwing him. I told him no problem, we would be more than happy to reverse the charges and send the bill directly to his employer along with the pictures of the room. He quickly declined and agreed to pay for the damages.

Let's see, so far, I have covered poisonous and those that bark, but how about those folks that have an affinity for other, more unusual pets?

In 1996, twenty years after our Arizona adventure began, my parents tore down most of the old mom-and-pop and replaced it with a beautiful three-story modern Franchise Flagged hotel. A couple of years later, my parents bought the mom-and-pop hotel next door and added it to my every growing list of managerial hats—as if I didn't have enough to do. It was your ordinary, cookie-cutter, two-story exterior corridor motel, again, with the home behind the front desk lobby. It only had forty units and had never seen a full room remodel or upgrade in its thirty-plus years of existence.

When we bought it, the plan was for it to go through an extensive renovation and become a new, beautiful franchised hotel. While waiting for all the plans, designs, franchising and financing to come through, we still needed to rent rooms. That meant we enlisted a team of our best, and we all rolled up our sleeves and jumped in, deep cleaning the entire property, cleaning drapes, shampooing carpets, new bedding and towels, scrubbing walls and bathrooms. In all honesty, even with all the hard work, elbow grease and new fluff, it was still literally embarrassing to rent these rooms. We kind of did it with a wince, a smile and an apologetic look. No amount of fluff and linen could fill the sagging centers of those beds. I mean, come on, you can put a new bra on sagging boobs and scrub them until they are glowing, but at the end of the day they are still sagging boobs.

When we finished the first week everything was looking pretty good, except for one room. It was a long-term stayer, who would leave occasionally for the weekend, and his room smelled just foul. Over his first weekend away we did everything to deep clean the room, just like the others. We left the room and thought, "Ha, Good Job!" I think we all succumbed to the definitive nose blindness. You know, where you are subjected to a certain offensive odor for so long you stop smelling it. But when the room was entered freshly the next morning, that thick musky odor hit you like a brick wall.

We snaked the drains and even checked the attic thinking, "Did something get stuck and die?" Nothing. Having no other ideas or recourse, we resigned ourselves to moving the guest and the need to start tearing into the walls to find it. Oddly enough though, the guest never complained about the smell. This is always a very bad sign. If something is obviously amiss in a room that has been occupied for a while, like a gut-wrenching odor or an obvious bed bug infestation, then dollars to donuts, your guest is the cause of whatever evil is underfoot.

After Musky Man's first night back, the housekeeper came in and said she thought she may have found the answer to our foul mystery. I followed her to the room. On the way she said she thought maybe mice were trapped under the bed. She had heard scratching and noises when she went to change the sheets. With that wonderful insight I called maintenance to go with us, because there was no way in hell a startled mouse was going to jump out on me from under a bed. (I am not ashamed to admit that when it comes to rodents, I am no longer a feminist. I want someone else to trap them, kill them, catch and release. I don't care, as long as I don't have to do it.

Truthfully, it is one of the reasons I got married. Thank you, my love.)

The beds were the standard hotel type, where they were resting on an enclosed box. Musky Man's room had two queen beds, and he slept in one and just kept some of his belongings on the other. We all filed into the room, one after the other, and waited, intently anticipating the sounds that would reaffirm the housekeeper's suspicions and my fears. After a few minutes of strained listening it started; faint scratching and scurrying sounds from under the non-sleeping bed. Maintenance and I looked at each other and then cleared the items off the bed, lifted the mattress, bedding and all, and put it on top of the other bed.

Then you could really hear it, there under the box spring. *My God, we have rats* was the first thought in my head. The second thought was, *How the hell do we lift the box spring off and keep them contained?*

There was no easy way to pull this bandage off. Nope, we were just going to have to do as we had at this property since the beginning: jump in. Nervously and fully prepared to run or scream, I held the flashlight while the maintenance man lifted the box spring just a crack. No shrieks or screams when he did, just these two adorable little rodent faces curiously looking back at us. No, not rats, but rather two very rambunctious, energetic, inquisitive, foul little ferrets.

With that non-threatening revelation, we felt secure in tipping the box spring completely off the bed. When we did, the full force of the stench filled our noses, damn near making our eyes water. The ferrets had burrowed completely into the box spring and there was poop and piss and rotting remnants of ferret food everywhere. Mystery solved. As per the extent of the food, damage and excrement under the bed, this was obviously our Musky Man's idea for a ferret house while he was at work. Wow! What a unique and innovative alternative use for a boxed bed that I had foolishly never thought of before.

This all led to the birth of our original pet policy:

- $10-$25/pet/day
- All pets must be kenneled when guest not in room
- Any pet disturbing another guest will be removed by animal control
- 25-pound weight limit
- No poisonous or dangerous pets or animals
- All of the above are at the discretion of management

Believe it or not, we didn't charge Musky Man a dime or throw him out, reason being the previous owners either never went in his room or didn't care. Either way it enabled him to perpetuate his putrid zoo. What was shocking was that Musky Man had not succumbed to his own toxic arrangement. We asked him to make other arrangements for his furry little ferret friends and he did. We gutted the ferret house and he moved to a much more pleasant-smelling room for the duration of his stay.

Just when you think you have seen it all—from a crazy cat lady who travels with all fifteen of them, to people who travel with their snakes and even monkeys—someone throws you an even bigger curveball. Every day we go over our front desk logbooks to see if anything needs to be addressed.

On a beautiful, bright, already stifling Arizona morning, I was going over the logbooks and incoming reservations when...

Beeeeeeeeeeeeeepppppppppp!!!!
Sorry to Interrupt This Chapter...No, Not Really

I guess I could have put this in the context of a regular chapter. It would have fit in the one called "Personal Responsibility" or it could have gone in the first God forsaken chapter; you know, the one about 100% Satisfaction Guaranteed bullshit. But I am not. I stopped and put it right here, so you would absolutely know how my life and how this shit really works. Maybe it will reinforce that the hotel business is twenty-four hours a day, seven days a week and 365 days a freaking year.

Most businesses, owners and employees get to shut their doors and take a break from their clients and customers, for the night or weekend. Hell no, not hoteliers or their teams. No holidays off for us. I guess that's not completely true; most of our team members get to go home at the end of their shifts, walk out the door and not worry until their next shift. If you are a supervisor, manager or owner of a hotel, though, you are on 24/7/365. It's kind of like emergency services personnel, without the cool equipment, uniforms or the glory.

Perfect example: it's seven in the morning and I am home, in my jammies. I haven't showered yet, haven't seen my husband or kids in days, because of all of our screwed up conflicting schedules, and I am sneaking in some writing time, trying to achieve my life-long dream of being an author. That's when my cell phone goes off like the damn bat cave phone.

Yep, you guessed it—it's my front desk team member at one of the hotels, and she has a guest who doesn't want to be charged for her room. Of course, the next logical question is "Why?" Her response is, believe it or not, a new one. One I hadn't heard over my more than forty-year career.

A lady was at the desk ready to check out and she didn't want to be charged for her room because the semi-trucks parked behind the hotel made her sick all night. Silent pause while I formulated an appropriate response. I asked my front desk team member what room the woman had stayed in, and she said she had been on the third floor. I told her to go ahead and put me on the phone with the guest. She said it would be a minute because the guest was busy dry heaving into the lobby garbage can. Nice picture and nice touch.

When Dry Heave was done unproductively retching, she got on the phone and, before I could even introduce myself, started recanting the horrific tale of her miserable stay with us. She stated that after checking into her room on the third floor, she decided she wanted to take in our majestic mountain scenery behind the hotel and opened the plantation shutters to look out the window. In doing so she noticed the three tanker trucks parked behind the hotel and immediately got horribly ill. Her eyes started stinging, her throat closed up and things just got worse from there. According to Dry Heave, her nose bled all night and she couldn't stop puking. She was absolutely convinced this was all because of the semi-trucks parked three floors below her room.

She asked me if I was aware that those trucks were parked back there. I said, yes, I was, that indeed there was designated parking for semis in the back of the property. Dry Heave then proceeded to tell me that she knew they were carrying sulfuric acid for the mines and that that was hazardous material. She knew this because she looked up the material number on the placards on the trucks and researched it.

I thought to myself, *Damn, that is some fortitude if you can forcibly puke your guts out past your closed throat, plug your continuous nosebleed and still be able to google that shit. Let alone read it with your stinging eyes. Impressive.* She must have been the freaking bionic woman or something. For a moment I thought that might really be true since she had also been able to read the hazmat number placards from three floors up that were on the sides—not the tops—of the trucks.

I asked her if she had noticed a leak or anything, given our team members had not complained or noticed anything, even though one of their entrances was between the trucks and the hotel. She said no, but she knew those trucks carried sulfuric acid and it had and was making her sick and she did not want to be charged for her room. She didn't know why we would even let trucks hauling poison park on our property. We were being irresponsible and putting all of our guests' lives in danger.

I calmly explained to her that acid trucks regularly moved through our city and other cities to facilitate the use of acid in the mines, and that those trucks were routinely inspected by

Arizona Department of Transportation and ran our roads and highways within state and federal laws and safety regulations. I assured her that their companies utilized all the hotels in town and had for decades without incident.

Hoping to calm her, I assured her that if there had been a sulfuric acid or fume leak, it would be quickly and obviously apparent, and more people would be ill. Dry Heave told me that there was no other explanation, and that I was being unreasonable. I did let her know that the flu was going around and that might explain her symptoms. With that, she yelled that obviously I wasn't going to do anything to help her and that it was fine because someday I would have to answer for this, to God.

No shit, this is how my days go. Hell, this is how my days, nights and weekends go. Take your pick. Like anyone, I have things I will answer to God for, but I do not believe—in fact I can almost guarantee—that this bullshit will not be one of them. Obviously, a God-fearing woman, so I couldn't tell her to FUCK OFF! Instead I started to say, "No problem, He and I are pretty tight," but she threw the phone back at my front desk team member before I could say anything else.

As she left, I heard her tell the front desk attendant that she was going to call all over town and let them know what we were doing here and then she was going to call the health department and the police.

Always wanting to be thorough, and, of course, interested in the truth, I asked my front desk attendant to have housekeeping call me after they had stripped and cleaned the room, and to make sure one of the supervisors was with them when they went in. About a half hour later I got the call and asked the obvious questions. Their answers did not surprise me but did succeed in aggravating the shit out of me.

They had stripped and cleaned Dry Heave's room, and you know what? No vomit anywhere—no puke in the trash can, no puke in the sink, no splatters around the porcelain throne, no foul smell. Must have been very focused episodes of projectile vomiting. No bloody towels, no bloody tissues, nothing anywhere. But who am I to judge? Maybe she ate all the bloody tissues or took them with her to lay at the feet of the health inspector, or just maybe she was an extremely thoughtful person and washed out all the bloody, vomit-soaked linens, dried them, fluffed them, and folded them prior to check out. How considerate.

Yep, another hour of my life I can never get back and I wasted it having to deal with a lying one-percenter who was willing to put their and everyone's else's integrity on the line for eighty-nine dollars plus tax. Because that is the kind of shit that gets put on the World Wide Web reviews. Total bullshit. Ever the struggling optimist and needing to find a shred of silver lining just so I didn't go off my own deep end, I thought to myself, *At least I got another story out of it.*

Now Back to the Regularly Scheduled Story

I would have thought that all my encounters with animals during my career would have been with live animals. WRONG, WRONG, WRONG. So very wrong. In no career, aside from law enforcement or military, do you think that someone at your workplace will ever come up and tell you they think someone has been killed. Let me tell you, if that ever does happen to you, nothing will get you out of your seat faster. Well okay, maybe someone screaming *Fire!* but nothing else.

On what should have been a routine Monday morning, it happened to me. Why I would think any day would be "routine" is beyond me. With that kind of wake-up call, who the hell needs coffee? I walked briskly with the room attendant to the room, saying a cheerful good morning to guests we passed in the hall, all the while trying to keep my composure.

You never want to run; it panics your team and the guests you encounter. It didn't matter, my mind was racing fast enough to make up for my feet, going over all the gruesome scenarios that could have led to what she had found and thinking, *That damn GM call center will not have a training scenario for this shit.* On that note, I was correct.

The housekeeper stopped short of the door, more than happy to let me go in first. Nervous did not begin to cover how I felt opening that door, and the feelings were not unwarranted. I couldn't believe what I found: blood and guts filling the bathtub at least two inches deep.

At first, I thought, *Oh my God, what the hell happened in here?* But then I started to take in the scene around me. Among the blood and guts were little bird feet and heads and tiny little feathers swirling around us from the draft of the open door, like the ice dance scene from a movie I love. Hunters had come from out of state to hunt quail—and to obviously gut and clean them in our bathtub.

This group of guys had come all the way from New York to Podunk, Arizona to hunt one of the cutest little birds you ever saw. Honest, if you haven't seen a quail, google it and see for yourself. They are adorable. The Bird Brains had spent a small fortune on plane tickets and out-of-state licenses. In fact, they had forgotten their licenses at home, and we helped arrange to get them their proper documentation so their trip would not be in vain and they could still go hunting. Who would have thought our kindness would have been repaid with me scooping bird innards out of a bathtub?

I guess in New York City, bathtubs double as cleaning stations, and this is just something I was not aware of. Isn't that what one would have to assume, given they eventually discovered they did not have one, and thought to themselves, *Gee, what would be the next best thing?* Do you think Bird Brains would ask that question at the desk, so we might have set up a table and hose outside in close proximity to the garbage dumpster?

Hell no, that would be just too goddamn logical, not to mention considerate. Instead they just added an alternative use for a bathtub, and gutted and cleaned their kills inside where there was air conditioning. Of course, since Bird Brains had paid for their weekend's stay, and their stupid asses paid a fortune to kill these little birds, this type of cleaning must be expected and included in the price of the room.

I am standing there just cussing in my mind and screaming the question in my head, *Jesus H Christ, what the hell kind of third dimension do I work in?* I coolly asked my room attendant to please go get me a bucket and gloves and to please call maintenance to meet me in the room.

I spent the next hour scooping out guts, rinsing, cleaning and sanitizing that damn tub myself. You ask, why did I do it myself? While those damn one-percenters sure as hell didn't pay for this type of service or use of the room, I also didn't pay my team members enough to clean up this type of twilight zone shit.

You would also think that in my career there would only have been one run-in with dead animals, but no. There seems to be three common themes in this book: One, fuck off, second, I am very often wrong in my assumptions of common sense and human decency, and lastly, rarely does anyone ever tell me the whole story the first time.

It was another "ordinary" Monday and I was reading front desk logs to catch up on the mundane issues that may have occurred over the weekend. It was again a bright beautiful day but this time it was a cool crisp fifty-degree Arizona winter morning, and I was snuggled up in one of my favorite sweaters. Mondays, it seemed, were a good day to discover that you had hosted dead animals or kills at your hotel. This would've been because more people hunt over the weekend. Turns out Monday morning readings of the logbooks were either completely boring or morbidly exciting.

Boring would be the ordinary things, like declined credit cards, third party reservation issues, guests needing extra towels and toilet paper. That is exactly how this Monday seemed to be chalking up, and I had started foolishly thinking that just because I had not received any emergent phone calls over the weekend, all had been well. Keep in mind my team had called me a number of times over the weekend, for all the mundane crap listed above. *No bells and whistles on this Monday,* I thought, as I aimlessly read through the handwritten notes of our well-trained team.

Stop. There it was, interrupting my calm and forcing me to stop and reread one entry: "The guest asked if it was okay if he brought his trophy elk kill into his room, because he was afraid someone might steal it out of his truck. I said yes."

Lord the things that made me go hmm and forced me to question the decision process of both my customers and team members.

Now, it didn't matter where you were from and whether you're a member of PETA or the NRA, you knew the images that the words "trophy elk" conjured up in your mind. Images of a more than eight-hundred-pound animal and a rack of antlers that could have more than a six-foot spread on them. The guest was afraid it would be stolen out of his truck, which means it was not fully contained within his full-size truck bed. Immediately I thought, *How did they get that in here and, in doing so, how did they get the rack through the door and in the room without damaging our walls or doors?* I urgently dispatched maintenance to check the hallways and room.

Most of this, I realized, was my own stupid, naive fault. What made me think that I didn't have to address dead animals as well as the live ones? In all fairness I had not trained, nor did

I think I would ever in a million years need to train, our team in what to do in the circumstance of a guest wanting to bring the bloody heads and/or carcasses of very large dead animals into their room and in doing so through the hotel. Thus, the following addition to the pet policy:

- All animals must be alive and be a commonly accepted domesticated species
- No disemboweling of animals or fish in the room, dead or alive
- No temporary or overnight storage of dead animals
- If there is any question regarding these policies, you must notify management immediately

I incredulously asked myself, *Do I really have to add this to my damn policies? I must or I wouldn't have hosted a dead trophy elk. What to do? Would I simply add this in writing for the guest to sign, put it in the employee handbook or just train for it in orientation?* I couldn't believe that I even had to consider and weigh these options. If I added them to the pet policy, what would our customers think was happening in our hotel rooms? If I included it in our orientation and employee handbook, would team members not return after signing that they understood this policy? In the end, it was only used as a training scenario, so neither our guests nor our new team members would think we were completely out of our fucking minds.

CHAPTER 4

THINGS THAT GO BUMP IN THE NIGHT!

(BATSHIT CRAZY OR GIFTED?)
(HOW TO DEAL WITH THE UTTERLY RIDICULOUS COMPLAINT)

Paranormal activity or legend was no stranger to our valley. How could it not be, when one of the original highway numbers into town was the dreaded Devil's Highway? Besides that, east of town, we had the devil's triangle out on Heckle Road, a desolate stretch of dirt road where people disappeared or suffered great misfortune.

West of town there was what the locals described as a "fold in the world." The state highway mile markers jumped from number 314 to 326 in the span of what was a mile on both sides of the highway. No explanation, no other numbers out of sequence, just missing twelve miles of the universe. The state has never replaced the missing markers. This is where the eerie heart-pounding music would be playing. Love a good ghost story.

I do believe that there is a higher power than ourselves, and that we all have a soul or energy that we come from at conception and return to after death. I believe that no one knows the exact name, nature or identity of this force and that we all practice faith, peace or religion where and how we are comfortable doing so. That is until we die, when we will all know, one way or another, who was right. The rest of us I guess will just be screwed.

Sorry to disappoint all the ultra-conservative Christians out there (which I guess includes me, being a cradle Catholic), but I am not arrogant enough to think I know enough about our vast Universe to say I am right or judge anyone else's beliefs. Nope, we are all just guessing and going with our gut. Now don't get me wrong, I am rarely without my Saint Jude's medallion or prayer card, and I always have a rosary. I am faithful but I do not go to church every week, or even every month, though I was taken to church every Sunday of my young life, and attended a high and tight Catholic school until my parents moved us to primarily mormonville Safford, Arizona. My Grandma Geraldine's greatest fear, other than crashing through every bridge she ever drove over, was that we would all be converted.

My Grandma Gerry was, by far, the most faithful, wonderful

woman that I ever knew. She was one of those rare individuals who not only practiced her religion on every occasion at church, but she lived it even outside stained glass laden, regimented, hallowed walls. She never had a bad word to say about anyone and loved even the sinners. I owed my albeit far from perfect commitment to staying Catholic and my dedication to Saint Jude to her sincere and unfailing example.

Her husband, my Grandpa Earl, joined the military during WWII, even though he had five children at home. He was kicked in the head while still stateside, during training. His buddies threw him on his bunk and left for weekend liberty. When they got back, my Grandpa was still where they had left him. The Army sent Grandma a telegraph notifying her of his injury, that he had been through brain surgery and was in a coma. My grandmother started praying to Saint Jude, asking for his intercession. (For those of you who aren't Catholic, this is just like asking your friend to put in a good word for you with the boss.) He was moved to different VA hospitals for treatment and more surgeries. When he was "close" to home my Grandmother would drive five hours each way on the weekends to be with him. Eventually he woke up, but he would never be the same. It took fourteen years of rehabilitation, love, faith and prayer, but he did come home, which was all my grandmother prayed for.

It is because of my grandparents' story of never faltering faith that I am the faithful person I am today. Faith to me is not defined by going to church every Sunday, even though she did, and I probably should. I knew many people, in all religions, who obediently went to church on Sunday, and sat in hard pews professing their faith, who were complete assholes the rest of the week and treated others like they weren't as worthy as they were. It is how you live your life and how you treat other people. Not saying I never doubt, not saying I never fail—I do both those things, just like we all do.

Then I touch or catch a glimpse of that medallion or prayer card, and I am reminded what faith and love really mean, and how hard and elusive they both can be. I try harder, I pray harder, I am kinder. I know that there is something bigger than me, bigger than my trials, bigger than my blessings. Because of this I know there are people like my grandparents who are genuinely more in tune with these faithful or frightening energies or spirits than others and that it legitimately can either be a gift or a curse. Most people don't ever get to meet one of the gifted, let alone wait on one of them. Luckily enough I was blessed to interact with a self-proclaimed clairvoyant in my career.

What seemed like an ordinary, middle-aged woman checked into our newly remodeled, forty-unit motel and uneventfully checked out the next morning. During her stay she never communicated that anything was amiss. At check-out she was asked, by our front desk attendant, how her stay was, to which the woman had nothing to report. One would think all was well. Again, let's say it together "I was Wrong!"

A few days after she checked out, I received a fax with a customer complaint from franchise. A formal complaint requesting a full refund, one of those that, if not answered in a timely manner, would result in the dreaded $150 fine. When these ominously foretelling faxes would come across the machine with their telltale beeping, you knew exactly what they were because of the form that painstakingly, gratingly rolled out of that cursed machine. These always made you cringe just a little until it finished, and you could read the latest version of "I May Be a Whiny, Lying Ass, But I Still Want a Refund". After this one though that beeping sound would literally make my stomach start to twist, as I wondered, *What the hell now?* and a prayerful exclamation of *Please make it stop!*

Impatiently snatching the wicked form from the fax machine's laboriously rolling jaws, I saw the name of the uneventful guest, researched all of our communication logs and found nothing out of the ordinary. The ill-fated fax told a different story. The complaint read:

"Shortly after checking into my room I noticed a bump in the bathroom floor and knew something was wrong. I am very in tune with the spiritual world. During the night I started getting the feeling that someone had been murdered in the room. I felt that maybe a trucker had beaten a woman to death in the room. Because I am so sensitive to this, I didn't get a good night's sleep, as good and evil were battling it out in my room all night. I feel this should have been disclosed to me at check-in and since it wasn't, I didn't get a good night's sleep. I feel I shouldn't have to pay for the room."

You have no idea how many times I read that damn thing

before I finally called my trusted GM hotline and asked, "Really? Really?" True to their blowing-smoke up-your-ass attitude and not-taking-any-sort-of-responsibility-for-a-damn-thing policy, the "specialist" responded by telling me, professionally and courteously, that they realized the complaint was unfounded, but I would still have to answer the guest and come to a satisfactory conclusion.

My stunned retort was, "What did you just say? Did you just tell me that you agree with me and you know that this is basically horseshit, but I still have to waste my time and respond?" The answer was a professional and sincere "Yes." Realizing this was an exasperating and futile path, I sarcastically asked if they had any advice on how to address this effectively. They apologized and said they had no reference for this type of complaint and that I should be courteous, and to please remember that my response would have to include an apology.

Hell, I didn't even know how to respond to my own GM hotline specialist, let alone the Gifted Guest. I just stammered through an incredulous "Thank You" while all the time screaming in my head, *Apologize for what?* as I hung up the phone. After I stopped pounding my head on my desk and, hoping to garner some advice or guidance from anyone and everyone, I showed the complaint to my supervisory team members. Surprisingly, no advice and the same reaction I had: "Really?" Then laughter. I did get at least one "Are you fucking kidding me?"

This was from Becki—to call her my right hand would

diminish how important she is in my life. She had been with us for a decade by then and had herself seen and heard a lot. She started out as our head housekeeper when we opened our newly constructed first franchised hotel and had since worked her way up, through front desk supervisor, and was now in charge of purchasing and accounts payable. We were married to first cousins, so we were family, through and through. (Told you I wasn't kidding about the small-town gene pool.)

Becki was no nonsense and had been blessed with an abundance of common sense. She could tell you if someone overcharged us a nickel and she took care of our customers the same way. If they were overcharged, undercharged or not charged at all, she knew it. She took care of us and them with equal ferocity and loyalty. I knew it was all me, though, when her filter broke during her response.

Like a man—or, in my case, a woman—adrift on the ocean, I was on my own. I slowly made my way back to my office, weakly attempting to delay the unavoidable call, rereading the complaint, hoping for an epiphany. Hell, I couldn't even figure out what the damn bump in the floor had to do with anything, let alone the rest.

Then, like turning on a light switch, it came to me. I formulated a plan and steeled myself for the inevitable phone call. As I dialed the number on the form, I was silently praying no one would answer. Not my luck, the Gifted Guest answered her phone on the second ring. I introduced myself and let her know I was responding to her complaint. She quickly recounted her story and was, to her credit, effectively distressed by the events of her stay.

I reassured our Gifted Guest that I understood and did truly realize some people had the unnerving ability to feel greater things than most and that this gift can lead to very disturbing and uncomfortable feelings. I let her know that I had lived here since I was ten and was not aware of a murder or death at this property. However, that did not mean it hadn't happened. I sympathized that a trucker could have murdered someone and just taken the body with him and no one would have been the wiser.

To address her anxieties even further, I let her know that this property had recently gone through a floor to ceiling renovation and before it was re-opened, we had it blessed by our local priest. Given her recent disturbing experience I let her know that we had already called the priest to come back and bless that room (in fact the entire wing) in an attempt to appease any energies or spirits that had become agitated. In closing, I thanked her for letting us know so we could address the situation completely and thoroughly for any future Gifted Guests.

In total I spent thirty-five minutes on the phone with this lady and in the end, she thanked me for not calling her a nut job. You have no idea how difficult it was for me to keep my composure and not, myself, go off the deep end. Altogether there was another hour of my life I would not only never get back but was spent calming and reassuring the Gifted Guest. We both ended the call on a good note; her, because I didn't call her batshit crazy and me, because I realized no matter how unraveled a guest might seem, and no matter how ludicrous a complaint might be, I could learn something. And you always, always, always need a plan. My amazingly discerning husband would just tell me to play into their damn crazy. He says doing just that had saved him more than once from having to fight or chase someone on duty.

No shit, I carried this complaint around in my purse for six months, because I knew no one would ever believe me, and I was positive this shit couldn't possibly happen again. This was about the time I started telling myself that one day I would write a book" There are two phrases I try desperately to keep from crossing my lips, because sure as shit, no sooner do the words spill from my mouth, then God or the Universe expresses their sense of humor and screws with me. One is "Now I have seen everything" and the other is "I will never see that again."

Yes, I foolishly thought I would only experience one of these ghost and goblin customers in my career. As per the emerging and repeating theme of this book I was wrong again! When I first received and read this next review my immediate thought was, *Did this lady come back after fifteen years?* Nope. Two completely unrelated people. Both "gifted", but to my knowledge, unrelated. This review I kept taped to my desk for a year, for the same reason I had kept the first one in my purse. No one would ever fucking believe this happened once, let alone twice. Hell, I didn't even believe it.

This time it wasn't Monday, and I wasn't reading the logbooks. In all honesty I couldn't even tell you what day it was. Now thanks to our wonderful technologically advanced world of social media, I was in the franchise system program that tracked customer reviews and feedback and allowed me to answer multiple outlets in one place. Franchise required that I log in at least every other day and respond appropriately to any possible comments, complaints or reviews. The days would run together until something out of the ordinary happened. Like this day.

The Ghost and Goblin guest in question this time was surprisingly a man, and he in fact had posted the review on an internationally recognized travel review site. The review was titled by the guest "Haunted." I thought, *Not again*. The man stated that he knew our hotel was haunted because the dresser drawers in his room kept coming out, on their own. (He had video.) His story continued that every time he closed them; they would slowly roll out again.

Feeling uneasy about this, he went down and told the front desk attendant what was going on. According to him, the front desk attendant, supposedly, let him know that sometimes strange things happen and offered to move him to another room. He knew that the hotel must be haunted or had been built on or near an ancient burial ground. He declined the offer to move rooms and wrote that he simply asked the spirit to leave him alone, and the spirit obliged.

All those third-party travel and review sites gave you an area to respond to your reviews and some of them graciously delayed the posting of our responses in lieu of approval. This was one of the sites with the approval delay. Which meant you couldn't cuss, request that the guest contact you directly or use any wording that blamed any third-party site. Again, completely ass backwards. Freedom of speech and deflection at its finest. I wondered what I could do or say, how I could respond effectively without sounding like the bitch that was doing laps in my head? I thought to myself, *I need a plan.*

First, I pulled out the communication logs; nothing. Next, I called maintenance and requested that they bring a small level. When they got to my office, I let them read the review and asked them to go to the room and check out the dresser for level and any other possible issues, as we all knew the ancient burial ground option was not a legitimate possibility. Given our dresser drawers were those ones on rollers, my money was on the level.

My dad was a millwright, welder and machinist by trade prior to losing his mind and moving to Arizona. One of the many lessons that we learned from him was that if something wasn't working right, always look at the simplest, most obvious reason first. Then go from there. You would think that this simple, common sense type of wisdom is how everyone would think. Mainly because it saved a great deal of time, money and, in this case, humiliation. Sure enough, when maintenance returned, they proudly affirmed that the dresser was slightly out of level, thus the drawers rolling out. They shimmed it up and, magically, the ancient spirits of rolling dresser drawers were gone.

I responded to the review by the Haunted Guest, and for the second time in my career thanked a guest for making us aware of a possible haunting. I took my time and reassured the guest that to my knowledge there had never been an ancient burial ground on this property. That the land on which the hotel was built had been a cotton farm for all the history that I was aware of, and that no evidence to the contrary had been found during excavation for the hotel. Again, I went through the whole blessings-prior-to-opening thing. In my response I let him know that we had discovered that the dresser had been slightly out of level and that the issue had been resolved with common sense and a couple of shims. BAM!

It was too late; he couldn't take it back. His words were out there for the whole digital world to see. I could have left the logical explanation out—not. I could have let him retain his glorified explanation—not. No self-respecting man where we live would have ever put that kind of review out there and opened themselves up to the possibility of utter humiliation and embarrassment. Just as he hadn't considered an alternative, more logical, explanation for the drawer, I don't think he thought that his comments would be called out with logic and common sense.

My husband was such a great sounding board when I was confounded by the male guest. This scenario I couldn't help but run past him, as he always had the amazing and exceedingly rare gift of common sense and thinking before he spoke. On my way home, we met up for a quick dinner at our local Chinese place. I gave him the scenario of the rolling drawer, without the Halloween embellishments, and asked him what might cause this. He looked at me for a minute and his first question to me was, "Did you check to see if it was level?" I couldn't help myself, I threw my arms around his neck and hugged him, giving him a well-earned kiss and said, just short of a scream, "Yes, Yes, Yes." He looked at me curiously and asked for the rest of the story. He knew me so well.

Let me reiterate I am not discounting the paranormal and I do believe that spirits or energies surround and interact with us. In fact, one of the properties I managed for over twenty years was inarguably haunted. We had team members that would not work on the third floor of that hotel and guests that would not stay on that floor. During certain months the spirit would become quite active and we did have the place blessed on more than one occasion. It was very real, and we knew exactly who it was. I myself experienced the spirit more than once and so did my team members. Some of the activity was even caught on camera. But that would be another book.

Two unbelievably, undeniably, amazingly similar stories with two very different responses. Remember, when faced with utterly ridiculous and completely unfounded or crazy reviews or complaints, do what my common sense-filled retired cop of a husband says to do: Play into their crazy. The Gifted Guest didn't really want a refund, she just wanted someone to validate how she felt and what she had gone through, even if it was only in her own mind.

Haunted was genuinely easier to address. He had given us something specific we could investigate, where Gifted Guest's complaint was more obtuse, it was just a feeling. I couldn't apply a level to and shim up a feeling.

While it could be argued that common sense could be applied to both scenarios, we all knew common sense didn't necessarily work when it came to anyone's feelings or emotions. In those instances, I tried listening, applied empathy and offered an alternative solution, even if that entailed calling in a priest.

For the customers reading this, please apply some common sense *before* you put yourself out there for the world to wonder about. If not, your words may come to bite you in the ass, regardless of how gifted you think or feel you may be.

CHAPTER 5

ASSHOLES, PREJUDICE AND DUMB-ASSES

(WHITE, BLACK, BROWN OR PURPLE WELCOME, JUST NOT STUPID.)

Such a heated subject, one that has caused more hate, pain, injury and death than we all would like to admit. You would think that coming from a small town, I might be racist or prejudiced, but this time you would be wrong. I told you that my parents raised us differently. They raised us to know people by their character and integrity, by their words and actions, not by their appearance, not by their faith, not by their race, not by their gender, and not by their orientation.

I believe there should be a mandatory course in high school regarding prejudice. Not to explain or define it, but rather to experience it. You know how they dress people up to be fat or a different race or a different age or different sex. Yes, everyone should have to do that. They should add one though. They should also make people physically challenged, blind or have a shocking disfigurement. Teach the world how to be empathetic and it just might be a better place.

In high school I got to experience being different firsthand. You know how your parents tell you not to do something, then you do it, it goes bad and you think, *Damn, I shouldn't have done that?*

My parents always told us not to ride in the backs of pick-up trucks. But hell, this was rural Arizona, everyone rode in the back of a truck. So, one day leaving school when I was fifteen, I took my friends up on their invitation for a ride home and jumped in the truck bed.

There were seven us in all, three in the cab and four in the truck bed. I was sitting down inside the driver's side tailgate, just happy not to have to walk the two miles home. It was Gary's truck. We'd been friends since seventh grade.

Gary guided his truck down the dirt canal road between the school and a cotton field, without a care in the world. Suddenly, he plowed into the car in front of him and everyone in the truck bed was thrown out of the truck—that is, except me.

Everything happened in over-exaggerated slow motion. I flew and hit the top of the truck cab with my face. Instinctively, because I was a musician, I hadn't put my hands out to break the impact. On the way, my left knee cracked into a cinderblock that was in the truck bed. I was never sure if I lost consciousness. I just remember hearing people screaming at me, not to move, not to get up, people yelling for someone to call an ambulance. There were panicked voices all around me, but I couldn't see anyone.

Within minutes we were at the emergency room doors and I heard voices again; urgent voices, people ordering others around. Someone grabbed my arm, and another grabbed my legs to turn me out of the seat. I made an unrecognizable sound to let them know that they were hurting me. They picked me up and laid me out on a gurney. I was rolling.

At our rural Arizona hospital, there were no CAT scans and MRIs—just X-rays and stitches. Couldn't be too bad, they didn't even send me to a hospital in the big city. After I was settled in my room, the doctor came in and told my mom that it would be okay, that my face was just swollen from the impact and that if she wanted to she could take me to a plastic surgeon in six weeks or so when the swelling went down. Mom worriedly asked, "Why can't she open her eyes, why can't she close her mouth?"

With the charm of a true chauvinist, he reassured my "overly anxious" mom with a condescending, "It's just the swelling, don't worry. Her front teeth are all broken from the impact but that can be fixed later too. She just needs time to heal. We will keep an eye on her and if all is good, we will send her home in a day or two". With that he was gone.

Barely a day after going home, my mom contacted a plastic surgeon in the city. When we met with him, he concluded that I had the worst facial injury he had seen in his twenty-two years of practice, and that had my mother not contacted him,

I would have been permanently disfigured.

The first time I saw my face, after my initial surgery, all I saw was a kaleidoscope of purple so dark, it was almost black, with shades of deep green and red. My teeth were jagged points, my nose had a rod that went straight through it, impeding my sight on the left side. There were two oval-shaped pieces on either side of my nose with what looked like metal staples going through them into my nose. There was an incision scar going from eye to eye across the nearly non-existent bridge of my nose. My nose only stood about an eighth of an inch high, even with all the metalwork trussing it up. My left eyelid drooped, and my eyes blinked not quite in sync with each other. But I could see. Well, okay, given my vision, I could see ten feet in front of me, but I could see.

It took over a year to put my face back together. I continued going to school. My old "friends" faded away, like my tears, and I found one or two true friends. During that time, I spent countless lunch hours in the library reading and checking out books. I thank God for that librarian and my band director. I found refuge in the books, and respite in my music. I found the meaning and value of friendship. I lost the person I was and learned who I didn't want to be.

That is why I had little patience for prejudices—except for a couple of perfectly justifiable ones. I do hold a couple well-placed and well-deserved prejudices in my heart, and those are the prejudice against stupid people and utter disdain for people who want to use their difference alone to garner sympathy or accuse another of treating them differently, when they are doing stupid shit. I don't like stupid. I have encountered more of these than you know. This is probably the hardest chapter to write because there are just too many to pick from, from short and sweet to long and harrowing.

Let's start with short and sweet. My team once called me over to one of our properties because they were having a problem with a room that wouldn't check out. I looked at my watch; it was already two o'clock in the afternoon and check-out time had been at noon. They had tried, in vain, multiple times to call the overdue guests. Overdue had answered the phone once and when asked if they were going to stay another night, they just hung up the phone and then refused to answer any further phone calls. The head housekeeper said she could hear the television going and music, but no one would come to the door when they knocked, and the dead bolt was engaged.

A quandary, hmm. I looked up their info. Two people registered, credit card valid and an out-of-town address. I had the front desk girl ring me into the room...no answer. I tried calling the cell phone listed on the room info...no answer. No clues about their stay and nothing extraordinary in the logs. The morning front desk attendant was not the one that checked them in, so no information there.

I drove my not-so-happy ass across town to the property that called me, to handle the situation or solve the mystery. The out-of-options front desk attendant had a key waiting for me on the front counter when·I arrived. Impatiently, I headed to the second-floor room and knocked on the door. Sure enough, no answer. I knocked a second and a third time, each time a little louder, a little harder. No answer. Don't you just hate being ignored? I know I do. As the last resort, I used the master key and the door light flashed a taunting red—the deadbolt had been engaged.

Next step. Banging on the door and yelling that if they did not answer the door, I would call the police and have them forcibly removed from the room. What I am really thinking is, *Holy crap, don't let them be dead, or hurt.* I was genuinely scared that maybe something bad had happened and we were going to have to break down the door to rescue, resuscitate or recover, and that's an awful feeling to have.

Praying this wasn't really the case, I banged on the door again, with the same threat as the first. Nothing. Hoping the third time was the charm I went to bang on the door again and, what do you know, the door is thrown wide open by a pissed off twenty-something girl with a hand on her hip and an annoyed-as-hell glare. She met my gaze and spat out an obviously irritated but unwarranted "What?"

Overdue is a young, pretty, maybe college-aged African American woman and there was a young man, same ethnicity and roughly the same age, lounging on the bed behind her. Obviously, Overdue and friend were both alive and well, so I told them they needed to vacate the room, that check-out time had been at noon.

The young man didn't even get off the bed and no one made a move to start packing. I peeked under her arm and the room was a mess and neither of them was even dressed for the day. So, I repeated myself, this time a little more forcefully. She finally removed her hand from the upper part of the door and with exaggerated disdain, walked with baby steps towards the main area of the room. They both finally begrudgingly started moving and gathering their things. While packing, they proceeded to call me a racist bitch and told me that the only reason I was doing this was because they were black.

I told them, "No, I am doing this because you should have checked out at noon, three hours ago. You could have requested a late check-out or, at any time, answered the phone or the door and requested to stay another evening. You should have answered your phone. You should have answered the door."

Overdue came right up to me with a finger in my face and told me I was only doing it because she was black. I told her "No, I'm doing this because you're acting stupid."

It took them twenty minutes to pack their shit and clear the room. I stood there the whole time listening to them berate me, call me names and cuss at me. As they were leaving, I thanked them for their business in the nicest voice I could. What I really wanted to do was smack them or ground them like insolent teenagers with smart mouths. In my head I questioned, *What the hell is wrong with people? How is this my fault?* I had never seen them and had no idea what race or age they were when I was knocking on the door, and, finally, screaming an ultimatum.

Let me tell you, if Dumbass or Entitled ever become a protected class of individuals in this country, I am in deep shit.

Because of the 24/7 nature of the hospitality industry, my phone was always next to me, always charged and always on.

Sure enough, it rang around one thirty a.m. one Thursday morning, waking me from a blissful sleep. Never a good sign when the phone rings at one thirty a.m.—not for work or personally. Since my husband was next to me and all my children were in bed, it kind of narrowed the options.

Sleepily I saw it was one of the hotel numbers and regrettably but dutifully I answered with a very groggy "Hello." It was my very new, very aggravated front desk team member. She told me there was a problem with a room and the guest didn't want to move. I inquired, "Why, what's wrong?" I was informed that the toilet was broken in his room, maintenance was already there, said the guest needed to move rooms and he was refusing to do so. As I had done so many times before, I said I would be right there.

I got up, threw on some clothes, ran a comb through my hair and assured my sleepy husband that it was okay, he didn't need to go with me, and that I would be right back. On my twelve-minute drive into town I couldn't help but keep going back and forth as to why she sounded so aggravated. Was it the uncooperative guest or the fact that she was scared shitless to call me at one thirty in the morning?

Upon my arrival, I ascertained again that pertinent facts were left out of the telephone story. The front desk attendant directed me to a room on the second floor. I grabbed a luggage cart to help the guest move, and headed to the room, hoping I could be the voice of reason or persuasion, whichever would have the desired effect.

When the elevator doors opened, I was greeted by my, also

very annoyed, maintenance man, who had been called out, and was dressed in shorts and a T-shirt. He told me the guest was drunk and didn't want to move rooms. I asked him what was wrong, and he let me know the toilet was broken and couldn't be fixed until tomorrow. Fair enough, but still not enough information.

I knocked on the door and entered the room just inside the threshold. The six-foot five white guy loosely rolled off the bed and miserably failed in his attempt to quickly approach me, like he was sober. He stumbled his way to the door and held onto it as if it would magically keep him from passing out. With his first slurred words, I could tell he was more than a little intoxicated, and he reeked of alcohol. Through mumbled speech he tried to assure me that everything would be just fine. The spit flowed freely as he made his mostly incoherent argument for not moving until the morning.

About the time he was telling me it was not that bad, my maintenance man pushed open the door to the bathroom. The movement caught my eye, and I turned my head, instinctively blurting out, "What the..." but stopped myself before the "fuck" came out.

The toilet wasn't just broken—the entire toilet tank was gone. Really, the whole tank was broken off and in pieces on the floor. There was a bowl and that was it. Towels that had been placed by our exasperated maintenance man covered the floor. He told me Toilet Tipper said he went to go to the bathroom, stumbled backwards and broke the toilet. To the guest's credit, at least he called the front desk and let them know. After taking all this in, I informed the guest that yes, he would indeed have to move rooms.

Incredulously, Toilet Tipper started to argue with me that it would be fine, and he would move in the morning, blah, blah, drunk and bleary-eyed blah. I patiently waited for him to finish, as I needed to harness and constructively direct my sleepy anger. If I had been taller, I would have grabbed him by the ear like a defiant child.

But I didn't. I told him in a stern and no option other than this voice that: Yes, he was moving rooms, and no there were no other options, because when he woke up with a hangover in the morning or when his drunk bladder got full and he needed to relieve himself, he would undoubtedly do it somewhere. He wasn't going to do that in a broken toilet and leave it for one of our team members to clean out, or worse yet, use an amenity whose intended purpose was not that. I told him that he had fifteen minutes to pack and move his things and that we would help. He finally acquiesced and did reluctantly move rooms.

Maintenance and I did not leave the hotel to go back home until two thirty in the damn morning. If Toilet Tipper had just done what had been requested of him from the get-go, by the front desk attendant, we, including Toilet Tipper, would have been asleep in our own respective beds. But no, that shit—no pun intended—would be just too damn easy. Before I left, I charged two hundred and fifty dollars' worth of damages to the guest's room folio.

The next day I went to work with a smile on my face and a song in my heart, which were promptly dashed when, later in the morning hungover, jackass Toilet Tipper, was now pissed off at me when he saw the charges. Another phone call, taking me from my work to address the customer's heated, whiny excuses. He wanted to know why it was so much. I let him know that because of the type of break, the entire toilet had to be replaced, and I had to pay my maintenance crew overtime to come out the night before to deal with the water, I was called in to address him not wanting to move, and the room had been taken off market for two days while the correct toilet was ordered and installed, and I had to pay staff to order, repair, replace and clean up his drunken mess.

Ah, his first tactic hadn't worked, so he then tried to negotiate with me. Rule number one and possibly two of successful negotiations is that one, you must have a defensible leg to stand on, and two, do not ask for the impossible. He had broken both of these rules and my toilet.

He wanted to know if we could split the cost. That is when I wanted to scream or laugh at him with, "What the hell would I do that for?" But I didn't because, that would not have been a professional way to handle that type of situation. Instead I pulled up my big girl panties and let him know that I could only charge him for half and would be more than happy to charge his company for the remaining balance and explain the reason for the charge and the circumstances surrounding it.

I inquired as to the correct contact person for this type of thing, as we only had the information for the main corporate office. Oh wait, what is that? Crickets chirping? A changed tune? What do you know, Toilet Tipper paid the bill for the damages on his personal card and on a separate folio. Stomped out. Never stayed again. Thank you, God. I went skipping back to my office with my blue birds and bunny rabbits.

Not mentioned yet in this book is the fact that my strikingly handsome and streetwise husband is Hispanic and was an amazing police officer, truly one of the good guys. Yes, I am and always will be a proud LEO (Law Enforcement Officer) wife. Both points will be significant in this next story.

A very sweet and very good-looking middle-aged lady, who was a regular guest who came to visit her husband in one of the prisons, came to the front desk and requested to be moved in-house from one of our exterior casita rooms. I asked if everything was okay, since she always requested those rooms and I was concerned something was wrong.

She said no, just that some young men with a Latino rap group that were staying at the hotel had approached her and extended an invitation to a party in their room later that night after their concert, and they told her there would be a lot of booze and good weed. Not being into that at all and not wanting to deal with the noise and possible party goers she just preferred to move inside.

With those words, my mind went from zero to *Oh shit* in one second. My head filled with thoughts of how to process this and ways to protect our hotel and guests. My brain screamed in silence while outwardly, I calmly made her a key and arranged to have her moved inside.

There was a concert at the local fairgrounds with several groups, and some of them were staying at the hotel. The concert was supposed to be that night and wouldn't end until midnight or so. I needed a plan and I needed one quick.

By the time the concert ended I had four security personnel and myself on site. Someone was at every entrance to the main building, with instructions that if someone didn't physically have a key to a room and their name was not listed as a registered guest, they were not coming in. Our local police department had been notified that there may be a potential problem.

As midnight approached, everyone was in place and thoroughly briefed, and I was intently watching the video cameras, nervously anticipating the nightmare that may unfold. Sure enough, shortly after midnight our parking lot started filling up like a trail of fire ants taking food back to the colony. By twelve thirty, they were parking across the street because we had run out of room. We were ready— or so I thought.

No one was exiting their vehicles. There were over one hundred and twenty carloads of teenagers and party goers. Then they started arriving, the entertainers in their wrapped SUVs. With this, a unified mass exodus out of the vehicles began. We thwarted any invasion into the main building but had failed to protect our casitas adequately.

As we were telling the incensed groupies and party hopefuls that they needed to leave the premise, they would ask us for their money back. We learned the rap groups had charged all of these people fifteen dollars a head to attend the "after party." Great for them; for us, not so much. Try telling two hundred and fifty to four hundred partygoers you don't have their money, it is not our party and it isn't happening—not here, not tonight.

By now we had called for backup and the police were in the parking lots persuading, then ordering people to leave. One of the great things about a small town is that most people still afford the officers the respect they deserve.

By the time we cleared most of the parking lot and got out to the casita room, the furniture had all been moved to one side of the room, a bar had been set up on the dresser, and there was a keg of beer iced down in our bathtub. Quite a few of the kids that the officers were kicking out weren't even old enough to drive, let alone drink. These young hopeful party goers had their backpacks with clothes, fully prepared to spend the night. Not happening at our place. Hell no. Over my dead body.

You know the African American rap groups that had requested the main building, were cool with our requests, respected our plan and understood. Not a disrespectful word from them and they were allowed to have a guest or two to their room. They hosted without incident and didn't try to talk us into anything more.

The entrepreneurial Latino group, which you had to respect for their ingenuity, was the group in the casitas. They were treated with the same respect as the rest of the groups and had been asked to abide by the same guidelines. The police were collecting IDs and had the group that was registered to the room, outside, given someone was supplying alcohol to minors. The spokesman for the group, was a maybe twenty-year-old skinny kid, with slick black hair and an attitude bigger than his brain. The Mouth was cussing me and screaming that I was just doing this because they were Mexican, that I was just a racist bitch, and so on.

The officers did not try and intervene, as they knew I could hold my own, and that time and karma would shortly be well served upon this mouthy young man with the misplaced anger and focused albeit limited vocabulary. It was all I could do not to give him back what he was giving and scream at him to shut the hell up or slap him for being the ill-mannered, disrespectful little shit he was being.

See, my husband worked for the county, and this call was out of his jurisdiction, as it was in the city limits, so city officers had rightfully responded. When it got as big as it did as quickly as it did, the county was dispatched to back them up. So just as The Mouth had begun screaming at me that I was a racist bitch, up pulls a county police cruiser, and my handsome, wonderful Hispanic husband walks towards me, leans down, gives me a kiss and asks me if I am okay. Eric did nothing but look over at The Mouth and then back at me and tell me that it looked like I was having a fun night. He then went to speak to the officers to see what they would like him to do.

The Mouth who, moments before, was calling me a racist bitch and blaming me for his screwed-up night and possible charges, suddenly changed his tune like a music box being opened. He couldn't apologize to me enough and told me how he was just mad, and he hadn't meant what he said. It was surreal how quickly the lyrics changed from "Racist bitch" to "Ma'am."

We didn't push for any charges that night, we just wanted to make sure our guests and property were safe and so were our local kids. Once the party guests were gone, we told the police that if the guests behaved themselves, they could stay the night, including The Mouth.

Party goers left, pissed but gone, the police left, guests were in their rooms and our team was hanging out just to make sure all was quiet. Looking out across the parking lot from the window in my sales office, I saw the same racist bitch-spewing guy walk outside and proceed to take a piss on the wall of our building. Yes, the one I just asked the police to cut a break to.

That was it, I was done. I cut him a break and he pissed on my wall? Kiss my ass. I called the police back and had them all thrown out, thanks to their, I-like-to-pee-in-public leader. And of course, The Mouth claimed it was not their fault; rather it was my fault, and where were they supposed to go, and they had paid for the rooms, etc. I politely told him they could use some of the fifteen dollars per head cover charge they had collected from the disappointed misled partygoers to pay for a room at another hotel.

Key to this story: Do not open your mouth if you are assuming anything about anybody. Unless you know, then check yourself before karma comes and bites you in the ass. In this case, when his pants were down.

Sometimes you learn from very smart stupid people just how stupid you are. Well you are until you encounter them and then you gain well deserved, hard-earned real-life knowledge. You know, prejudices are not simply defined by race, as I have found "stupid" in every race or ethnicity, and "stupid" is also not reserved for any particular age group either.

Remember the hotel I said we cleaned to the best of our ability in order to rent rooms prior to renovations? Well, some of the first guests that we rented to were a couple of young, sun-kissed, shaggy-haired young men, travelling across country in an old van. They were friendly and polite and had told us they were taking a break from college in California to see the country. Uneventfully, we rented them a room and gave them the keys. Within thirty minutes they were back at the desk and courteously reported that the air conditioner in the room wasn't working. Given we weren't full and it was the middle of summer in Arizona, we sincerely apologized, had them sign a registration card for a new room, gave them the keys and collected the old ones.

Their new room was just a few doors down, so they wouldn't have to move their things very far. How considerate of us. The faulty A/C was logged in the maintenance book to be looked at and the room was taken off market until they did. All bases covered and guest happy. When I left for the evening all was well.

By the next morning that would all change. As I pulled into the parking lot for work the following day, I noticed Cali Kids plus six going in and out of the old and new room, tossing their belongings into the van. Yes, a bright burning light bulb moment. How could I have been so stupid?

We hadn't gone to the old room and cancelled their keys. They had simply thrown the door latch, leaving the door to the old room open, and about eight people had used both rooms. Now I could have simply chalked this up to a lesson learned on my end, but I decided to make it their lesson as well. After all, why not spread the knowledge?

I charged both rooms on the card we had on file. I watched and waited anxiously at the glass entrance door, both folios in hand, hoping they would come to the desk to check out. The stars aligned, and they did come to the office when they left. I handed the Cali Kids both folios and thanked them for their stay. They took them, not realizing that they weren't duplicates of the same folio. At least not yet.

They tossed the paperwork in the back of the van when they left. One of the free- spirited, arm pit hair-growing, let's-travel-across-country-on-someone-else's-dime ladies in the back must have finally read them and the van braked hard just after it was put in gear. Doors flew open and in came Cali Kids and friend to ask about the charges. I explained to them that I saw them coming out of both the rooms when I drove in this morning and that they must have just forgotten to let me or the desk know that the A/C inexplicably started working or that they had invited a few extra friends to stay the night. So, as a courtesy, I went ahead and took care of the appropriate charges and paperwork.

Now you think that just the fact that they knew they had been caught would have been enough to sufficiently embarrass them into leaving politely. Not the case. I listened to them rant about how I just didn't like young people and that I was doing this because of how they looked. On and on and on. I finally told them with a straight face and motherly calm that it wasn't how they looked but rather how they acted that prompted the charges.

Cali Kids and friend left telling me that they were going to sue me and that I would be hearing from their fathers' lawyers, and that I didn't know who I was messing with. I let them know that I would welcome any inquiry into the charges and reminded them that I did have valid signatures on both registration cards. They left in a flurry of middle fingers and misplaced youthful outrage. Never to be heard from again.

In this next story I am going to age myself, and I am sure several of you may not even know what Watergate was. Sad but true. For those who don't, it was the scandal that rocked our nation, ousted a president and sent a number of political higher-ups to prison.

Well, believe it or not, we were lucky enough to host a Watergate felon in our then country clubesque, perimeter wall you could walk over, at the base of a cotton candy cloud-topped mountain, local minimum-security federal prison. His family would come to visit him on occasion. When they did, we had the privilege of hosting them. They were a very nice "normal" family. I was just a kid then and I remember my mom talking with Watergate Felon's son. His son was the long-haired hippie type, with a guitar slung over his shoulder, wearing an army jacket and carrying a military style duffle bag. He was sweet and polite, and my mom took a liking to him. They would visit at the desk when they came into town.

Well, the day came that WF was released from prison, and his family was there to welcome him home. I remember him coming to the desk, shaking my mom's hand and thanking her for the hospitality shown towards his family. Then he did something that raised the ire of my mom. He apologized to her for the appearance of his son.

I was so proud of my mom when she looked him straight in the eye, and while still holding his outstretched hand, firmly told him that no apology was necessary, that his son was a delightful and polite young man, however, given that he himself had just gotten out of prison for one of the biggest scandals in our country's history, he might want to apologize for his own behavior. With that, my mom turned around and walked out of the office and into her private quarters. She was seething, and Watergate Felon excused himself to me, turned, and walked out the door.

This all goes to prove that in my experience, stupidity has no bounds and knows no race, no gender, no age. It's an equal opportunity affliction. Rest assured though, I will rent you a room and wait on you no matter your race, no matter your ethnicity, no matter your size, no matter your faith, no matter your gender, no matter your orientation, no matter whom you love, no matter your appearance. In the famous words of my father, everyone's money spends the same. Even assholes and stupid people.

CHAPTER 6

DO YOU KNOW WHO I AM?

(WHAT'S IN A NAME?)

A name means a lot. When it is written on paper, it reflects your training, your education, your dreams or, very possibly, your criminal record. I am a firm believer after perusing customer name lists for more than forty years that some people: 1. Hate their children. 2. Have a very twisted sense of humor. 3. Were high as hell when they named their kids and 4. Never thought they would end up marrying that urge fulfilling one-night stand or "I have such a nice friend" blind date.

Why the hell would you even date a man, let alone marry him with the last name Head and then hyphenate your last name to include your maiden name of Goode? It's bad enough that your business card states the last name of Goode-Head, and you aren't in the sex industry, but you decided to have children and send them to public school. What kind of sick bastard are you?

One of my favorite things to do was to read over the incoming guests' names. Some you couldn't pronounce on your best day and would hope their first name would be usable and then you could skip the Mr. or Ms. So-and-so and just go right to the familiarities. This one last name had twenty-six letters in it. Unfortunately, the first name didn't give me any relief from the impending oral slaughtering of the guest's name. When they arrived to check in, I just simply asked them how to pronounce their name. Their answer didn't help, but I asked and then, properly defeated, promptly defaulted to Sir. It's all I could do not to ask him if he had any children and offer my sympathy to them and their kindergarten teachers for having to figure that out.

And then there are the names that make you smile, or you just can't believe are real. We had one regular who worked for one of the legal justice systems and would come down at least once a month. I could never bring myself to say her surname out loud and would only call her by her first name. I am sorry I just couldn't bring myself to say, "Thank you Ms. Name-of-an-80s-porn-star and I hope you have a great day", or at least, not without laughing. How could I say that with a straight face?

The greatest one was a hoot to say, though. Most of the time with the tongue-twisting, dirty mind-inducing names that I heard, I was left wondering why the hell wouldn't they change their damn name? I mean, you will find no bigger fan of family pride and honor, especially when it comes to the family name, but when your last name is any possible spelling or pronunciation of female or male genitalia, and you insist on telling everyone it should be pronounced somehow against all phonetic rules, well, you are just setting your kids up to be the butt of endless jokes and ridicule. Honestly, are you just that much of an asshole parent?

I will always remember this one though. It was so hilariously true that if it had been my name, I'd wear a shirt everyday just letting the entire world know what my name was, so they could go the rest of their day with a shitty grin on their face. If she hadn't presented me with valid ID I wouldn't have believed it and refused her for a fake. But no, it was valid. Her name was The Magical Dragon. (Name was changed to protect her true identity, but you get the gist of it.) In that order: First, middle, last. No shit. I always wanted to meet her parents and ask them how much weed they had smoked or were they dropping LSD when they were naming her? The name did suit her, as she always looked like a fabulous retro hippie herself.

I digress.

Nope, other than the examples listed above for personal entertainment, I don't give a shit who you are. I will treat you the same whether you are purple, blue, the richest or the poorest person we serve, short, tall, fat, thin, young, old, male, female, other, heterosexual, homosexual, bisexual, or any of the other whatever's you might be. Nothing used to aggravate me more than when people would utter the words, "Do you know who I am?" No, and I do not give a shit who you are!

In all honesty there was one more phrase that would garner the same amount of aggravation, and it always succeeded in raising my ire: "I know the owners." Jesus Christ are you really telling me that? Believe it or not, I know the owners too! And you know what? I have known them for forty-four years and I have been one of them for damn-near a decade and I have never, ever met you!

Oh, I'm sorry, I must have misunderstood your definition of the word "know". You meant to say, you looked up the owner's names and started throwing them around, or you stayed here once before six years ago for one night, and during that ten-minute interaction you discovered that we were long-lost soul siblings or related in our previous lives?

During that brief contact our connection was so profound that without the need for continued communication, we somehow both should fully remember the names of our children, grandchildren, siblings, where we went to school, how we lost our virginity, where we buried the bodies, and the skeletons in the closets. This imaginary enduring one-sided interpretation of our fast friendship entitles you either to a free or discounted room, or you are somehow allowed to treat my team like complete shit.

One of the greatest—or worst, depending on your perception of or perspective on this story—was a classic case of karma in action. If this story was on social media, it absolutely would have gone viral. It was one of the rare evenings that my husband and I were off together, given his rotating schedule and my crazy hours. We foolishly and naively thought we were spending it at the home of a friend, celebrating their housewarming. Better said, that was our plan. True to form, that's not how the evening worked out.

Only an hour into the lovely housewarming, my phone rang. Recognizing it as one of the numbers from one of the hotels, I answered it. (The hospitality industry really doesn't care if you are spending a pleasant evening catching up with friends over cold beer and good food, or if you and your husband are hoping to end the evening with some long-overdue sex.) Nope, crazy little hopes like that are dashed with the sound of a cell phone. This time though, it was far from mundane.

My female front desk attendant was sobbing hysterically. After calming her down enough to understand what she was trying to tell me, she said that the man in room #206 had come down to the desk, harassing her, interfering with other guests at the desk and had pulled her down behind the counter and tried to kiss her. "I'm on my way," I said. Click.

My husband saw the panicked look on my face and responded to the frantic waving of my hands motioning to the door. We ran out the door and jumped into our car, me relaying the short version of the story: Our team member had been assaulted.

I not only knew #206's name; I knew him well. He was the senior manager of a vast and well-respected international company that bore his family name. They did a large amount of business with us while they were in town working for the mine. He had stayed with us for years and had the looks of a Greek God. No kidding— chiseled features, brooding eyes, perfect hair, perfect smile, the perfect scruff, and a body that really did prove working out works.

Both he and other team members would stay with us on quite a regular basis. He would speak of his wife and kids and had always been nothing but a gentleman. There had never been an issue with his behavior before this, but his last couple of stays had been different. We had noticed some peculiar actions, like him starting to travel with a bodyguard, him answering the door to his room in nothing but a towel and tipping room service with hundred-dollar bills.

At that time, I had never been on a "ride-along" with my cop husband and had never experienced his skill at driving fast. It was impressive and terrifying at the same time. True stuntman status. I didn't know what scared me the most—not getting to my team member in time or getting killed in a fiery crash on the way there.

While I was trying desperately to press the nonexistent brake pedal on the floorboard, I had a death grip on the mother-in-law handle above my door. After calling the police to dispatch officers, I was on the phone with my team member, reassuring her we were on our way and making sure she was okay until we and the police could get there. I was a combination of pissed off beyond belief and scared beyond measure for her.

We and the officers got there about the same time. Only when I was standing next to her did I hang up my phone. That team member wasn't just an employee; we had known her and her husband for years and they were our friends, even outside of work. She was sweet and kind and in no way—as no woman would—deserved what Mr. Greek God put her through. That night, though, I saw her overwhelmed and shaken.

There was no one in the lobby, and for some reason it appeared to be eerily quiet. Odd how a circumstance could change the feeling of a place that you're in every day of your life. It seemed each word that was spoken was amplified against the silence. We all went behind the privacy wall at the desk to talk to her and find out exactly what happened. She told us that Greek God had come down to the desk around nine p.m. and was acting kind of out of character, saying inappropriate things, asking her when she got off and telling her he wanted a kiss. She reminded him that there were video cameras, in response he lifted his shirt, exposing his bare chest to the camera and said he didn't care.

She thought everything would be fine and he would leave her alone when another guest came to check in. Instead he started asking the new guest if he thought she was pretty. The new guest did their best to ignore him and they tried to give her cash to pay for their room. Greek God grabbed it out of her hand and gave it back to the guest, saying their money wasn't good here. Finally, Greek God walked away to the opposite side of the lobby and she was able to check in the new guest, finish the transaction and get them their keys to their room.

After the new guest left, Greek God appeared again and opened the rear entrance door to the area behind the desk. She had forgotten to lock it. He came through it and left her no way to escape from behind the front counter, unless she was going to leap the four-foot-tall marble barrier. He grabbed both of her arms and tried pulling her down to the floor behind the desk and started kissing her. She managed to stay upright and get away. When she did this he loosely—like he didn't have a care in the world—leaned up against the back wall under the welcome sign.

Thankfully another guest came up to get toothpaste and asked for a wake-up call. With that, Greek God casually walked out the same door he came in through and went back to his room. Everything hadn't quite registered and she was amazingly able to take care of the guest in front of her. Then the adrenaline and realization hit her.

She started shaking and crying but managed to lock her door and call us. She told us that after Greek God got back to his room he called down to the front desk. In a shaking insecure tone, she asked me, "Do you know what he told me?".

I said, "No, what did he say?" Trembling she said, "He asked me if I knew why he did that. I told him no". She said he responded with an arrogant laugh and said, "Because I can, they will fire you way before they will lose my business." I couldn't believe what I was hearing and hugged her again. We and the officers all reviewed the video surveillance and it proved the events just as she had stated. The officers asked for guest information and we were more than happy to oblige.

The officers, one female and two males, went to the room to do a "knock and talk", since they had seen the assault on camera. After continued and persistent knocking, Greek God finally opened the door and let them in the room, still dressed in the same clothes he had been in at the front desk.

Immediately upon entering the room the officers knew why he had been acting differently. Laid out on the side table in his suite was an abundance of cocaine. Greek God was either so jacked out of his mind or just so fucking pompous and pretentious that he didn't even attempt to hide it. He was promptly arrested and cuffed up right there and then for not only the assault, but now for drug charges as well.

In an utterly perfect example of small-town justice and karma, the female officer was the one taking him, cuffed and whining, through the lobby. "Why are you doing this to me? You are hurting me! Do you know who I am?" I was standing with my team member, shoulder to shoulder behind the counter, and listened with a satisfying grin, when the female officer told him in a wonderfully assertive, not-quite-bitchy, tone, "Because I can!". You have no idea how thoroughly rewarding and utterly vindicating that was for myself and more so for my traumatized team member.

Sometimes it is all in a name. Remember, I was raised where your family name was something you took care of. Greek God obviously didn't give a shit about his family name that literally was his company. In all fairness, yes, I know it was the drugs talking and it was the reason for his behavior that night, but he chose to start doing drugs. No one forced that shit up his nose. He did that all by himself and it changed him, and not for the better. I know I went all serious on you for this story, but it really was funny as hell witnessing karma kick his ass so swiftly.

There were some customers though, you looked forward to

waiting on. They were the ones that made it fun and rewarding, and I don't even think they realized how much they enlivened or brightened our days. Every day we would go through incoming reservations looking for special requests or anything out of the ordinary; someone needs extra pillows, there's an anniversary, they needed a rollaway or a crib. All manner of ordinary things, but sometimes it didn't take something huge to turn ordinary into extraordinary.

There will always be names that I love to hear or read, just because remembering that customer brings a smile to my face. We had one very special customer that at the writing of this book, was still staying with us, after twenty years. His name was Buster, or rather, that was his nickname.

Everyone knew him, and I didn't know anyone that didn't like him. Some may have thought he was a sexist arrogant ass, but that was only when he drank, and even then, you knew he really was harmless. If any one of us girls had ever taken him up on his tipsy half-hearted advances and flirtations, he would have run the other way. We would feign indifference or insult, and he would tone it down a notch, knowing he had gone just a little too far.

He really was a good man, a dedicated husband and a loving father. We knew his wife, and he adored her. We knew that he loved hot dogs, so much, in fact, they were part of his travels and his retirement plan. So dedicated to hot dogdom was he that we named a hot dog after him at the restaurant. He had a hell of a sense of humor with eyes that reflected his hearty laugh and ever-mischievous smile. I was only maybe thirty or thirty-two when Buster and his partners in crime— or wait, co-workers—started staying with us.

Buster had stayed several times and he was jovial, to say the least. One night he and his buddies were out on the patio enjoying a cool breeze, sipping back cold beers and cocktails, winding down a smoke. I went out to say hello and buy them a round. We were all just throwing around some small talk when one of his guys told me a story about Buster at a huge industry golf tournament. Never know what you're going to here when the liquor is flowing.

Let's just say Buster worked for company B and Company A was the biggest competition in their market. Well, both companies had a two- or four-man team playing through, with Buster's team playing just ahead of the competition. Now Buster was a firm believer in three things: Hot Dogs are the perfect food, Liquor makes you do everything better, and All is fair in love and war.

Arizona is a damn hot place to play golf and so, it was perfectly understandable and justifiable that they were keeping themselves cool by fully partaking of the endless supply of complimentary ice-cold carbonated fermented hops. And what do you have to do when you are drinking volumes of alcohol and exerting yourself under a searing sun?

His buddies told me Buster peed in every hole after they retrieved their putts and before Team A was on the hole. Oh my God, I was laughing like hell and Buster just looked at me with that shitty grin and, with a true politician's heart, would not confirm or deny the story. I'll tell you one thing though it made me never want to take up golf.

He was predictable, and we knew what he wanted. He wanted one room and one room only when he came, and he didn't have to tell us which one that was. We knew that before he came. We switched out the pillows in his room for his pillows. (He liked his pillows flat, not fluffy.) We knew he would eat dinner across the street and bring home a hot cup of soup to his room when he was done. We knew he might call us at the drop of a hat and order twenty-five Buster Hoagies for the morning to take to the mine or he would reserve his table at the restaurant and be there in fifteen minutes with a crew. We knew he had a good heart. He is the perfect example of why I stayed in the hotel business so long. He was demanding and challenging at times. Yet he was constructive in his criticism when he needed to be, he was funny, respectful and appreciative. May everyone be like Buster.

Then there was the wonderful elderly gentleman that I will refer to as P.H. He came twice a year from the U.K. to look through his telescope and gaze into our clear Arizona skies. He was friendly in a stoic, very proper and dignified manner. He was a pleasure to speak with and was always gracious and polite, the perfect gentleman. He remembered our team members by name and just emailed us personally to make his reservations for him. He was a dear sweet man and we enjoyed his patronage for over a decade.

There was Ritchie, John, Bill, Anthony, Oscar...so many that, just seeing their names on the arrival list, made us smile. Even if something was wrong in their room or with their reservation, they brought it to us, we fixed it, they thanked us, and we tried our best to not have it happen again. They brought us something to eat or drink, and we would listen while they shared stories about their families. Stories that when you listened you knew how much they missed them. We made sure they had special treats in their room when their work put them with us instead of their loved ones over holidays.

There were cancer patients who came in for treatment, until we were notified that they had passed. Families in for weddings, anniversaries, graduations or funerals—we were there with them and for them, to help them, to make it easier to be away from home, to be away from their families.

These were just some of the names we knew and gave a damn about. There were many more we didn't know, but our team still cared and gave their very best. Those customers are the ones that made this job worthwhile and rewarding. We rented them a room, yes, but they left a piece of themselves with us, and took some of us with them. We called them "friend".

Thank God we had so many wonderful guests or I very possibly would have gone certifiable because of the rest. So please remember to make an impression with your name, leave a piece of the best of yourself so someone smiles when they recall it. Don't be the customer we cringe over when we remember you or refer to as the dick, asshole, jackass, liar or psycho, because you were so much of one of the aforementioned nouns that we didn't bother to even attempt to commit your name to memory.

CHAPTER 7

PERSONAL RESPONSIBILITY

(OR LACK THEREOF.)

Responsibility means what? That you are accountable, that your actions are within your power to control, or something close to that. Such a simple word— okay maybe not, as it seems quite difficult for some to master. Could be that a few folks have a hard time with it because the word has more than four syllables. Maybe it's me or us, and that we are assuming way too much, as to its simplicity and relevance.

You presume that when a school sends a sports team on a road trip with coaches and chaperones that there will be zero problems or, if there are any, they will be promptly taken care of. That would be the logical train of thought, but again I would be wrong, and because of this, would have to occasionally work in what was my continuously spinning whirly gig of an alternate universe.

So many nights I might as well have just not gone to bed for the phone calls that would endlessly wake me up. It was like I constantly had a three-month-old baby that needing feeding, burping and for me to clean up their shit. This night would be no different; I just didn't think the shit part would be quite so literal.

True to form, I got woken from a neverendingly hopeful restless sleep by my aggravated and desperate front desk team member letting me know that other guests were complaining about some kids running up and down the hallways, knocking on doors etc. She let me know the kids were part of a high school basketball team that we had checked in earlier in the day.

I was familiar with the team and had her ring me into the coach's room for the first time, to let him know what was going on. He assured me it would be dealt with. Just like a new parent that puts their now-sleeping baby to bed, I foolishly laid my head down on my cool soft pillow thinking all was well and I would now enjoy a blissful sleep.

Hell no. An hour later another call, same issue. I spoke with the coach again and let him know, in no uncertain terms, that if I needed to move guests because of his unruly team, it would be considered damages, and the school would be held responsible and charged for their inconsideration. I was again assured it would be taken care of. This time I waited, listening intently, waiting for the next cry of that cell phone. Silence. No other calls, all was well, I floated off to a peacefully naive and unaware sleep.

I was in my office, the next morning, when my head of housekeeping, followed by three of our room attendant team members, nearly burst through the door in my office with utter exasperation. You could tell just by their body language alone they were all pissed as hell. Again, not rocket science: Pursed lips, crossed arms or hands on hips, and eyes that were lit up (and not in a good way).

The head housekeeper told me through gritted teeth that the guests, teenage boys, in a couple of the balcony rooms were dropping bags filled with shit off the balconies and trying to hit our team members with them as they went in and out of the back entrance of the hotel.

Before I even had a chance to respond or get out of my chair to wring someone's neck, in an appropriate politically correct, pissed off and protective manner, of course, my laundry attendant suddenly appeared with the same indignance: someone had shit in both of our guest laundry washing machines. In reviewing the security camera footage, we only saw the teenage boys go in and out of that room the evening before, so not much doubt as to who did it. The same system showed bags dropping from the rooms above and hitting the ground, barely missing our team members.

That was it. I called the coach and demanded that he come down to the desk and speak with me regarding his team.

He came and seemed completely indifferent to what I was telling him, almost annoyed that I had interrupted him. It was basically, the boys had won, they were just letting off some steam and that was it. Lord I was pissed.

Team Shit was already checking out, so not a lot I could do, as they were leaving anyway. It wasn't like I could throw them out or anything. Then it hit me, but I didn't do anything just yet. After all, I needed to give them the opportunity to show their true colors or possibly redeem themselves in the final minutes of the game.

I waited until they left and watched as each one of those little defecating shitasses-in-training and the adults that were their poor excuse for role models left the hotel. I was waiting, and it didn't come. Nary an apology among them. I smiled with squinted eyes and a jaw set in determination as they left, for by now I had gotten used to having a plan.

It wasn't the end of their foul behavior; when my team checked Team Shits' rooms, they called me to one specific room and said I needed to see it in person. Never a good conversation. I got to the room and was waved in by my head of maintenance and housekeeping. At first, I didn't see anything horribly amiss. Then I noticed the upward glances of my team and I followed their steely gaze, knowing it would be bad. And it did not disappoint.

The ceiling of the room was covered—and I mean covered—in what had to be thousands of glistening wet spit wads. Now we knew what else they were doing when they ceased wreaking havoc on our other guests, our team members and our poor defenseless washing machines. The ceiling looked like one of those throwbacks to the 70s popcorn ceilings on steroids. It would take forever to clean it off and might very well have to be repainted or plastered when done.

The washers and the pavement had to be cleaned and sanitized, two team members quit, the ceiling had to be cleaned, sanitized and repainted, and I had to refund a night's stay to another guest. Fine, no problem. I had a plan to do a little extracurricular training for Team Shit & Spit.

Before they arrived back at their school, I had called the principal, the superintendent of their school and the board of education and let them know of Shit Team's behavior and the indifference of the coach, team and chaperones. I forwarded the statements from our team members, the refund to the guest, and pictures of what they had done, while out of town being an embarrassingly shitty representation of their school. Oh man, what a plan—and a pretty shitty pun.

It was three hours later when the phones started ringing. Calls from parents wanting to know which rooms had participated in this atrocious behavior. Before answering, I asked the logical question: Did they ask their child? They said they did, and the kids wouldn't say and because they wouldn't, the school was suspending the entire team.

So, let me get this straight. They wanted to know which rooms so they would know who did it, so their sweet angel wouldn't suffer the consequences? And they wanted my help to do it? Hmm, I had to think about that a moment. After deep contemplation and reflection, my response to them was, if the team felt they needed to go down together as a team, so be it. I had always been a staunch proponent of teamwork. None of them stepped up to the plate while they were at the hotel to do the right thing or stop anybody from doing the wrong thing.

With no further information to be garnered and no assistance being offered to the Team Shit & Spit's parents, I quickly transitioned from their saving grace to the utterly insensitive, uncaring bitch that didn't know what it was like to raise kids or be one and they were just having some harmless fun. Wow. You know I truly believe that the phrase "Fuck off" should be socially acceptable in the workplace under certain circumstances, and this time would have been one of those times.

Again, not one single apology from any of the parents, the coach never called back to apologize; only the principal and superintendent, which was appreciated but unnecessary, as they weren't the ones that did anything wrong. As far as the parents and coach go, well, I guess the apple didn't fall far from the tree.

I sometimes wonder how many of Team Shit & Spit's team members ended up in prison or getting their arrogant little asses kicked by someone who just wasn't going to take their "shit" anymore. Will the puns ever cease? They all got suspended. Not sure what happened to the coach; however, they were banned from ever staying at our hotel again. In the end, Team Shit & Spit -0-, Team Insensitive Bitch -1-.

As I have previously stated, Arizona is hot as hell in most places, so guests often rent rooms to do things like a mini vacation just to swim and get out of the heat, or just to float, ha-ha. I loved having local folks come and rent a room to enjoy the pools and fun with their families. In fact, I encouraged it. The key to everyone's happiness—especially my own—was that everyone that used the pool would be a paying guest.

One beautifully clear and incredibly hot Saturday afternoon I was driving by one of our properties and noticed quite a few vehicles parked on the east side of the building, which was closest to the only exterior entrance for the pool. This would be unusual because, in our market, most of our business was Monday through Thursday. The guests that were there over the weekend, not all the cars— at least not ten—would be grouped together like that. What are the odds?

Being the Nosey Nellie that I was, I did a U-turn, pulled into the porta cache of the hotel and went in to see what was going on. I said hi to my front desk team member and headed straight to the security camera screens and noticed that there were twenty people in the pool, with one of the lounge chairs blocking the interior entrance to the pool.

I asked the front desk attendant if they knew who was in the pool. She told me that one of our team members was having a party for their child on the patio. I knew about that. The front desk attendant didn't know if the rest were registered guests or not. Not that they had been trained to notice something like this, not that they had been trained in how to intervene when it happened, not that they had been trained to call me, but hey, who was I to judge the rest of a story I was never informed of?

I went to our team member who was only using the outdoor patio, having a great little party for their son and said hi and wished them well. They were cooking hot dogs on our outdoor barbeque, eating cake and enjoying the day. I asked them if the people in the pool were their guests. The answer was no. I wished the little guy happy birthday and said hi to everyone with a friendly smile, hiding the suspicious bitch now formulating a plan in my ever-whirling little mind.

With that I went around and tried to open our interior entrance to the pool and couldn't because there was what looked to be about a ten or twelve-year-old boy laying on the lounge chair blocking the door. A couple of chairs over sat two women, lounging and having a conversation. There was another child on a lounge chair between them and at least ten other people in the pool, kids and adults. I again tried to open the door, to no avail.

Keep in mind this door was glass, so they could see that someone was at the door trying to get in. True, I was dressed in jeans and a baseball shirt, as it was supposed to be my day off and I was supposed to be spending my time joyfully grocery shopping. So, for all they knew I was just a guest trying to get in to use the pool I had paid to use.

Finally, I was able to open the door about an inch and asked through the crack for them to please move the chair so I could get in. They looked at me, but no one made a move to get up. Not the kid, not the adults, no one.

Round two, I again opened the door a crack and asked if they could move out of the way so I could open the door and get in the room. Again, blank looks in my direction, but no one made a move to get up or move the furniture. I saw them talk to each other and could hear them, so I knew all parties were not deaf, mute or unable to speak English. Round three and round four all went the same, and still nothing.

I needed a plan but was sufficiently pissed off and proceeded without one. I pushed all my weight—and I am no little girl—against the door and, inch by inch, managed to push the pool lounge chairs, along with the unwavering, rude adolescent boy, across the floor and away from the door. While doing this it subsequently moved the rest of the furniture as well.

The two ladies sitting there were suddenly shocked and incensed that I pushed open the door and moved the lounge chair that their precious twelve-year-old was on. According to them, I could have injured him. Screw me or that I could have injured myself forcing open that damn door.

Straightening my shirt, regaining my composure and staying calmer than I would have even expected, I apologized, identified myself and explained that it was the only way I could get into the room, as my repeated verbal requests were completely ignored. I informed them that the furniture needed to stay away from the door so that other guests could freely access the pool area. I asked them if they were guests of the hotel. They said no that a friend of theirs that used to work there had said they could come use the pool any time. Really?

I let them know that this was incorrect and if they were not a registered guest of the hotel or one of my current team members (who would have to accompany them to use the pool), they would need to leave or they could rent a room and continue to enjoy the pool.

Well, I guess that just flipped the bitch switch, mainly because they got caught and were now embarrassed in front of their family and friends. Not my fault, although at least one lady believed it was.

Just as they did not make a move to open the door, they did not make a move to start leaving. I reiterated my position and made my request again to the same blank stares. I was thinking to myself, *Do you work for the customer service help line? I have seen that look before.* Nothing. So, this time I let them know if they didn't start leaving, I would have to call the police.

Miraculously, as I have found to be true over the years, when I mentioned the police, everyone finally started gathering their things, except one of the original Lounge Ladies, who was comparable in size to me, but a little younger. She proceeded to come towards me aggressively as I turned to leave and go out the door. I thought if I could just get through the door, she would cool down and everything would be okay. I was wrong! Undeterred, she just kept coming and followed me out through the door and into the tiled hallway in front of the vending machines and elevator.

Unfazed, I just kept walking while she yelled after me to stop and talk to her. Wasn't going to happen. Then, adding insult to injury—or in this case, injury to insult—she slipped on the floor in the water dripping from her own wet swimsuit. Out of the corner of my eye, as I rounded the corner, I saw her go down. I took the ten extra steps to the desk to tell our front desk team member to call an ambulance, just in case.

Before I could even turn around to go back and check on her, she was at the desk, dripping wet and on me like a biting dog. She was now even more pissed, seething because she had added embarrassment on top of embarrassment. She was screaming at me about the nonexistent possible injury to the twelve-year-old, she was screaming at me that I had pushed her, she was screaming at me that I hadn't even tried to help her. She wasn't limping, crying, broken, bleeding or bruised.

She must have gotten up and continued to follow me damn quickly and effortlessly, as our team member hadn't even finished dialing 911 and she was screaming at me that they had permission to be there, and on and on. I listened and tried to explain that she couldn't possibly have permission from an ex-employee, as they had stated, because not even current employees could extend that courtesy to non-registered guests. Again, I offered to rent her a room. Nope. the calmer I stayed the more it seemed to fuel her fury. She wanted the fight and I wasn't bringing it.

This seemed to be the unwritten rule in so many of these situations. The calmer I stayed, the more it pissed the other person off, regardless of who was wrong or right. And there is no need to fight when you are right, dry and not embarrassed. So, she went to walk away and when she did, she picked up the cookies we baked daily and put out for our guests on the front desk and threw them at me.

That was it. Instead of dispatching medical response, they

dispatched the police. When the cavalry arrived, she was in the parking lot, half-dressed, half-dry and half-cocked. She wanted me charged with assault for barging into the pool and her slipping on the floor; or, as she put it, pushing her. At our invitation, the police viewed the security footage and promptly cited Lounge Lady for simple assault and trespassed her from the property.

Who would have thought that the cookies we put out to make our guests feel welcome and appreciated would then be used as a weapon? I was fairly used to acting as the pool police, but a cookie warrior? Not so much. Maybe that's how Cookie Monster started out; just a sweeter version of the bitchy deflecting Lounge Lady. Well I guess that's how the "cookie" crumbles. (Oh, come on, you know that was funny.)

There are some stories that bring a smile to my face instead of a scowl. One was during our monsoon season where we had endured two days of sporadic torrential downpours and wind. Rain that would start and stop on a dime and drop more water in fifteen minutes than a regular rainstorm did in an hour. Thus, the need for Arizona's large bridges over dry riverbeds. Flash floods abound during this time of year and we build the bridges the way we do for just that reason. Just like we get the bullshit, "But it's a dry heat" we get the "How come y'all have these big ass bridges and no water?" Never fails when someone says that, Mother Nature says, "Hold my beer."

This weather pattern tends to keep some of our customers from their appointed rounds. They are not like our postal service. You cannot do all the things you might need to do inside a mine during monsoon season, at least not safely. It turned that imposingly massive open pit into a colossal mud bog arena. No kidding, how would you like to hydroplane through slick mud and clay in a vehicle so big it's like driving a three-story building? Even worse, how would you like to be the poor bastard in the regular size service pick-up truck or van that got to play keep away next to that? Crews would sometimes return to and hole up in their hotel rooms, waiting for the weather to clear. Our community is two and three hours from the nearest big cities, so it's not like they could just go home. Instead their companies routinely had them wait it out.

Let's see, this time, eight guys between the ages of say, twenty and thirty-five, were cooped up in their hotel rooms, not knowing when the boss would okay them to go in. (Translation-no drinking.) My oh my, what could a body find to do to pass the time? Read a book, watch a movie, play cards, have a meaningful conversation? None of the above. Let's go shopping at one of the plentiful hunting and/or sporting goods stores. What could we buy? BB guns and targets, of course.

It was still too wet and windy to be outside, so they figured they'd set them up in the hallway of the hotel and shoot them down the hallway. This was all happening on the third floor, so we didn't hear anything. How would one suppose that we would find out what was going on? That would be when our housekeepers, who so innocently came out of the elevator to start cleaning on the third floor, narrowly missed getting shot.

The girls were rightfully pissed, I was pissed, so that meant it was someone else's turn to be pissed. I went up to the third floor and there was no one in sight. Not one Trigger Happy man, no targets, no telltale signs of anything amiss. Just mysterious silence. I already knew what rooms they were in, though. They were one of our drilling crews. I picked one of their rooms and knocked on the door. Nothing. I picked another room and knocked on the door. Aha, the hushed whispers of people trying to be quiet and failing badly.

Hint: Never try to hide from someone in a hotel if they have the option of making a master key and have access to the registration log. I knocked again and still no one came to the door. I knocked one more time, this time letting them know if they did not answer the door, I would just open it with my master key. Lo and behold, the door opened, and a very sheepish-looking twenty-something Trigger Happy young man stood before me.

With my index finger, I nudged open the door a little wider and their entire eight-man crew was crowded in the room like disobedient children hiding from a scolding parent. You know that look of, *If I just act cool, Mom won't know I did it.* None of them looked much older than my own son. With the best pissed off mom look that I could muster, I asked them what they thought they were doing, shooting BB guns off down the hallway. I let them know they almost hit the girls, knowing full well they knew that, or they wouldn't have all been hiding in the room like wayward naughty schoolboys.

The oldest of the Trigger-Happy Boys immediately broke my cop husband's cardinal rule and foolishly decided to be the spokesman. The spokesman said they were bored because of the storm and just thought it would be fun to get a couple BB guns, and didn't mean to do any harm, and that they were sorry.

It was everything I could do to not yell at them that they were grounded. Instead, I told all the Trigger-Happy Boys that this would stay between me and them for now, but if anything, else like this happened, I had the number to their crew foreman. (And if you knew him you would understand the power of that statement. He was demanding and didn't take any crap from anyone and didn't tolerate any bullshit from his crews.)

I told them I would be more than happy to make that phone call. It was up to them what that phone call would include. It would either be, what a pleasure it was to host his crew, or it would be to tell him that none of them were ever allowed to stay with us again and why. The choice was theirs. I gave them a bit of advice, though, which was, if you wouldn't do it in your own mother's house then don't do it in mine. For God's sake if they were that bored, we could have set up something in the breakfast or conference rooms, but to just shoot randomly down a hallway with blind corners? What were they thinking?

I maintained my pissed off mom face until I left the room with their repeated and desperate assurances that it would never happen again and their gratitude for not calling their boss. The grin came across my face later, after I left the room and was walking back down the hallway. They all looked like little boys who got caught with the errant sling shot aim or something. I couldn't help but think of my own kids and their friends at the house getting into mischief caused by boredom.

These were some of the guests that kept me so long in the industry. These folks would spend more time with us at the hotel than they did with their own families. We got to know them and interact with them, and they got to know us. It was nothing for one of them to ask us if we would take their uniforms to be embroidered with their names while they were at work or any number of other tasks or favors for them.

One of these requests for a favor stayed with my heart. We had checked in a crew for a long-term stay. They were with us doing a big project in the mine. There was this one mountain of a man. He had to be six foot five or more and every hardened steely bit of three hundred and fifty muscle-bound pounds. Intimidating in his build and size, but a quiet and gentle demeanor.

Every night we would put freshly baked cookies out on the desk for our customers: sugar, oatmeal and chocolate chip. When they were gone, they were gone. We noticed this Steely Gentleman always took a sugar cookie or two to his room with him when he came in from work, a friendly smile crossing his face and a quiet, gracious thank-you.

One evening their crew must have worked late and by the time they came in the cookies were gone. The Steely Gentleman looked disappointed but proceeded to his room to get cleaned up from his long hot day at work. Within about thirty minutes he was back at the front desk, showered and clean. He asked for me. I came out and asked what I could help him with. With his response I couldn't help but smile. Hell, I almost teared up.

He wanted to know if we could make him a dozen sugar

cookies, just for him, and asked how much it would be. While I was running pricing through my head, I asked him if he wanted them ready by morning, as I figured he wanted to take them to work for the crew or something. He told me no that he would pick them up when he got off work the next day. Maybe it was the puzzled look on my face or maybe he just wanted someone to know. That Steely mountain of a man told me he wanted them because he missed his mom and she baked him sugar cookies every week. Eating them reminded him of her and of home.

In that moment he looked like a little boy just missing his mom, just wishing he was home. In that same moment he was the epitome of a man, willing to lay his vulnerability out to strangers. I assured him that we would have his cookies when he got off work the next day, and we did. Against Sugared Steels' objections, I wouldn't take a dime for the privilege of being able to give someone a small taste of home.

Lest we end this chapter on a warm and fuzzy note, we should talk about paintball guns and how a hotel room is no place to host a paintball war. That sentence probably has you thinking, *She has got to be fucking kidding*. Nope, not kidding. In fact, I don't joke around a whole lot at all. I've been told by more than one person that I was just born old and am way too serious. It's true, this profession has jaded me, and in the end, I had to marry my sense of humor.

One afternoon Becki my front desk supervisor and best friend, who, it was rumored, had even less of a sense of humor than me, notified me that my well-seasoned, experienced head housekeeper had called and needed me to come to a casita room; that there was something I needed to see. The whole way over, my little bitch starts running around in my head again. *What the hell am I in for now?* If she is rattled, I am going to be pissed off at something or someone for sure.

This time I had never been so right, although I'd have preferred to not be. I walked in through the door of the room into a 1960s tie-dyed art project gone horribly wrong. Splattering's of pink, yellow and orange furiously decorated the room. The white plantation shutters, the carpet, the furniture, the television, the phone, the walls, everywhere. Nothing had been spared. My first thought was, *What the hell?* as I tried to process the explosion of abstract art all around me.

It took me a minute to figure out it was a paintball fight gone awry. It took a minute because who in their right mind would ever think this kind of shit would happen in your hotel room? According to the registration card, it wasn't a bunch of errant teenagers either. The Reckless Rembrandts were adults. Well, I use that word loosely because again, what kind of "adult" did this kind of shit? Someone who never cleaned a hotel room in their life; someone who didn't realize I was going to charge five hundred dollars on their card for additional cleaning and damages, that's who. I knew they knew what they did was total bullshit when I never even received an irate phone call questioning or disputing the charges.

I mean were these Reckless Rembrandts high? Were they drunk? Or were they just such complete asses or so stupid that they thought, *Why not, let's play!*?

Remember a few chapters ago when I said I had only been called to a room one time to see how great it was? Actually, it was two rooms, but the same day and for the same tragically beautiful reason.

For quite a few years, we had worked with the foster child program in our county and a neighboring one by helping to host a conference for foster kids. Don't ask me now what the actual acronym was or what it stood for, because I couldn't tell you. But I can tell you what it was. The state would put up foster kids in the hotel, have a great dinner, let them swim, watch movies, have a snack night and listen to some lectures. It always made me happy and sad all at the same time, because it was for foster kids who were going to age out of the system and had never been adopted. They gave them a nice distraction before turning them out into the world. Kind of like a last meal, without the execution.

As an incentive to youth organizations, we routinely offered fifty dollars to the kids in whichever room had been kept the cleanest during their stay. The rooms would be judged by our head of housekeeping and the money awarded before they left so they could take their prize with them. Sometimes this incentive strategy worked, sometimes it didn't, and you might be surprised how and when it would and wouldn't.

This group was no different. We offered the reward and they notified the kids before they got off the bus. It never failed every year when these kids walked in the hotel, you could tell their defenses were up. They were wondering where it would come from and they wanted to be first on the draw. You know, the disrespect they expected and thus gave in anticipation. They expected judgement for their rainbow of hair color choices, or their piercings, their boisterousness, their shyness, or just because they knew we knew they had no family.

The first few hours between staff and kids were always rough and a little tense. They pushed the boundaries, we treated them with respect and dignity, calling them Sir or Ma'am just like any other valued customer, because they were just as valued. By the end of the weekend, the Sir and Ma'am would come full circle back to our team members and these children found their way into our hearts.

The morning they were scheduled to leave, the head housekeeper was inspecting the rooms prior to service to see who would be awarded the prize. I was wishing the kids and chaperones the best in the lobby and waiting to hear what room had won. My head housekeeper rang me and asked that I come to a room on the second floor. As I went up the elevator, I was praying to myself, *Please don't let something be horribly wrong.* (Like weed, damage, smoking, or any number of stereotypical things that went through my head.) I just didn't want that to be the case. The kids had all been so great. Please no.

When I met the head housekeeper in the room, she had tears in her eyes, and it didn't take long to know why. The room we were standing in looked like it had never even been touched. Both beds were meticulously made, as if no one had even slept in them. Hospital corners and linens so tight you could've bounced the proverbial quarter off them.

The bathroom was spotless, not a speck of trash in the cans or anywhere else. The end of the toilet paper roll had been folded to a point. They had even gone to the front desk to get extra amenities, like soaps and shampoo, and replaced what had been used, and what had been used was nowhere in sight.

If it hadn't been for the dirty towels that were folded and neatly placed on the luggage rack with a note letting us know they were dirty towels, I would have thought no one had stayed in this room the entire time. I looked at her and said, "Well, I guess we have our winner."

But she shook her head. There was another room, next door that was just as neat, and the rest were close. She couldn't, she didn't want to decide who should win; that was why she needed me.

We both knew it, without saying it: this fifty-dollar prize meant something to these kids. It meant more to them than it had to some of the entitled groups of kids we had hosted many times in the past. Schools, clubs and organizations that cost money to belong to or be a part of. Those kids rarely won, as it didn't always mean anything to them. Their parents had given them more than that as spending money for their trip. Now, I am not saying they were all bad, but the condition of their rooms stood in stark contrast to these. These kids belonged to a different club—one they would give everything not to belong to.

In that room we saw the pain and the pride of a child. We saw what they lived without and what they wanted to be. How could I possibly decide? So, I didn't. With room numbers in hand we went down to the lobby and announced how proud we were of all the kids and how they had treated our team, our hotel and their rooms. So much so that we could not decide on a clear winner and instead we were awarding two fifty-dollar prizes and thanked them for their amazing effort.

The kids were proud, they had earned our respect and their money. I hope they know that they forever made an imprint on our hearts.

CHAPTER 8

SUITE WEDDED BLISS

(KNOT!)

The summer between my junior and senior years, I worked a second job, to save enough money to buy my wonderfully crappy first car. I spent the interminably hot summer days building fire breaks, grooming hiking trails and cleaning outhouses for the forest service. I came home drenched in sweat, plastered in fine desert dirt and with just enough time to shower and change before running over to the diner to start my shift. That summer I was blessed with hard work, enough money for a car and the greatest blessing of my life. I met my future husband, Eric.

We had been dating for two and a half years when, just before turning nineteen, I discovered I was pregnant. I had driven the three hours from college, like I did every weekend to work at the restaurant, but this time it would be different, I was going to tell Eric I was pregnant. Only my best friend knew, and I was scared. On the seemingly endless drive home, the scenarios of his possible responses, looped over and over, in my head.

As soon as I got into town, I went to the diner to relieve my mom on the line. When I walked in, she was all smiles and sunshine and told me she just had to tell me something. She disclosed that Eric had asked my sister to go with him to pick out a ring and he was going to propose. I was never so relieved in my life. My fear and self-doubt disappeared. He didn't know yet and he wanted to marry me.

Eric and I have been married for thirty-five years now, and because of how I feel about him, I am an utterly hopeless romantic. My wedding was the farthest thing from extravagant or unique. It was 1985, the height of the union strike at the local mine, which meant no one had any money and tensions were high. My dress cost less than one hundred dollars and my attendants and I each carried only a single silk rose, purchased at the local five-and-dime.

We had no dance and only a few finger foods along with our wedding cake at the diner afterwards. By two in the afternoon, we were on the road to our California weekend honeymoon. The highlight of my wedding day, besides marrying the love of my life, was when I set my veil on fire blowing out my unity candle at the altar. Nothing could dim my happiness, not even the fact that our thirty-nine-dollar wedding bands, that we ordered out of the mail order catalog, had not come in, leaving us to borrow a pair of hideously scarred silver, turquoise and corral bands from a waitress friend of ours who had been married five times. Even the priest looked at them like, "What the hell?" when he blessed them.

I planned my first wedding in 1987, just two years after my own. Since then I have planned and coordinated more than one hundred and fifty weddings. I became the bride's advocate (or bitch for the bride). If the overbearing bridesmaid was insisting things should be done the way they were done at her wedding, I was there. If the narcissistic band member thought they should be the focus of the reception instead of the bride, I was there. If daughter had a different vision than mother, I was there. If dad wanted to pay for booze for his cronies instead of the dream flowers for his daughter, I was there.

Not to be satisfied with simply the talent for something I wanted to be validated with another piece of paper for my wall and sought and earned the privilege of becoming a certified master florist. While those classes like the hotel administrator training gave me the credentials and the proper industry titles and names for what I did, Polly really taught me everything I knew. She helped me develop and refine a talent for something I didn't know I had. Growing things had never been my forte, in fact I was notoriously bad at it; so bad I was surprised I was able to have children. I figured my challenges in the world of horticulture were Mother Nature's way of getting back at me for killing her beautiful creations to arrange them.

We had hired Polly in laundry but soon transferred her to the flower shop when we learned she was a very talented florist who had worked in California shops for many years. She grew up working piece work in the fields of California and could efficiently organize any project. Girls half her age couldn't do half the work she did or as well as she did it.

Despite our company dress code regarding extracurricular jewelry, Polly was always properly iced. At work she would be adorned with at least a dozen gold bangle bracelets, six pairs of earrings, three gold necklaces and six or more rings. Becky and I always joked with her that if she ever drowned her body would never be recovered because her jewelry would weigh her down.

Her silver hair formed the perfect short wave and her makeup was always soft and meticulous. She was fiercely spirited and loyal. If you were her family or friend, you were for life and she would defend and protect that with all she had. On the flip side, if she didn't like you, well let's just say it was rumored she kept a box cutter in her do when she was younger. I still want to be just like her when I grow up.

She taught me which flowers you should wire, which needed their stems slit with a knife or smashed with a hammer. She taught me how to build corsages and bouts, which I always hated, and she was insanely good at; how to make cut flowers live longer; and how to build stunning wedding bouquets and centerpieces, which were my favorite. We worked together so long and so well, we rarely spoke while doing flowers. We knew what the other one needed, and what flower to hand each other to fill a hole in a piece.

All this wedding work would lead to more than a story or two. You knew the Naked Cowboys could not have been my only encounter with wedded bliss. Occasionally, during one of the mind and soul numbing stints staying at the mom and pop for my parents, something would happen to break the monotony, make Eric and I value each other a little more, appreciate our marriage despite our odd circumstance and unfortunately justify my growing cynicism

Our kids had been asleep for a few hours and were soundly tucked in their little beds swaddled under the gables of the house, I grew up in, that also served as the office to our sanity hanging on by a thread, customer service world. That was when you could still live on property at a hotel as the manager. This arrangement was strange and trying for my husband, adventurous for my children and annoyingly frustrating yet reminiscent and familiar for me.

My husband and I had just gotten into bed and my grandfather's wooden regulator clock chimed a resonant even protest that it was midnight. As the last chime sounded, so did the annoying reverberating buzz of the doorbell downstairs. Someone was at the door. Given it was so late, my husband got dressed to accompany me downstairs. After all, it was after what I liked to refer to as the "asshole hour", and with no expected reservations, I never knew who would be at the door.

We trudged downstairs simultaneously trying not to wake our sleeping babies but plodding enough to resonate our annoyance. If it had been the first week we were there, the steps would have been lighter but given we were just past two months of this shit, the steps reflected our frustration. Our mood lightened some when we went to unlock the front door and found a young couple still dressed in their wedding attire and wanting to rent a room for their honeymoon.

How fun, the best reason we could think of to come downstairs. The Happy Couple were smiling and laughing and full of youthful exuberance. Him keeping a protective arm about the waist of his beautiful new bride and her holding onto her train and veil saving it from the ever-present Arizona dust and dirt. We did all the paperwork, got them their keys, gave them directions to their room and congratulated them on their nuptials.

On their way out, The Happy Couple asked if the restaurant across the street was still open. I let them know that it was. Away they went, happily walking hand in hand across the street. They left their "Just Married" streamer strewn car parked in front of the office/house window. My husband and I must have been struck or touched by their newlywed glow, because we sat down, next to each other, on the little couch in the lobby and started reminiscing about our own wedding. We got lost in our own romantic past, recalling stories of me setting myself on fire at the wedding and him completely forgetting to pack any clothes for the honeymoon.

Through our sentimental storytelling we heard yelling, and noticed The Happy Couple were coming back across the street, but this time it was different. There was no hand holding, and the streetlights did not illuminate any glow of happiness. We didn't think they noticed us in the lobby, as we had turned off the lights before we sat down. By the time they got to their car it was obvious that Happy Couple were no longer Happy.

From what we could hear she had wanted to stay at the diner across the street and have a few more drinks and he wanted to go back to the hotel and proceed with the honeymooning. An argument ensued. She managed to open the car door, but instead of getting in, came back out the door, toasting glasses in hand. She promptly threw them at him, calling him a selfish asshole as the glasses broke and shattered on the concrete.

At that he slapped her, called her a little bitch and tried pushing her through the open car door. My six-foot one husband, who had been raised to never hit a woman, stood up and banged on the glass door, making his presence known. He unlocked and threw open the door, fully willing to come to her defense. I was on the phone calling the police. This was prior to my hubby becoming an officer. The sight of him only resulted in a slight pause from the tipsy Happy Couple.

Unfazed, the battle continued; yelling, cussing and basically beating the hell out of each other. As my husband started for the car, the local police pulled in the driveway and whoot whooted their siren. The noise broke up The Happy Couple like ringing the bell for a heavyweight fight.

As the officer got out of his car to speak with the bride and groom, my husband came back inside. A few minutes later, The Happy Couple got in their car and drove to their room, the officer left and that was the end of it.

We just couldn't fall asleep after witnessing something like that. My husband and I tried in vain to calm ourselves by getting something to drink when we weren't thirsty, cleaning things that didn't need to be cleaned and organizing room keys that didn't need to be organized. (Yes, this is when we had real metal keys for each room. We kept two for each room, in the littles cubbies under the counter, and two extras, hanging above the key-making machine, in the closet across from the front desk.)

Soon enough we realized we weren't going to be able to go to sleep until we knew everything was okay with The Happy Couple. We walked out the back door and headed over to their room, listening for yelling or the sounds of breaking objects. As we approached their car, all appeared to be well and seemingly quiet. The only noise was the gently rustling leaves of the sun-weathered pecan trees that were in the middle of the gravel courtyard. Great, Happy Couple, happy again and all was well. Wrong.

Turning around to head back to the office, our babies and bed, we saw him. The groom was asleep in the front seat of the car tucked under the blanket of his tuxedo coat, his head resting between the less than comfortable head rest and the cold hard glass of the driver's side window. There was a faint light coming through the drapes of the room window, like the bathroom light had been left on as a reassuring, comforting night light.

The short-lived celebrity marriages of today had nothing on this Happy Couple. They hadn't even made it through their wedding night. Screw three days, three weeks or three months, Happy Couple hadn't even made it twelve hours. A little free advice here folks, and I don't care if you are rich or poor, famous or completely unknown: If you can't even make it through your wedding night, and alcohol was more important than your honeymoon, run. Run fast. Don't walk! Run to the nearest courthouse and get it annulled. Just cut your losses and run.

Sometimes it wasn't even our bridal party that gave us trouble. While we did host a lovely wedding this beautiful fall evening, I couldn't tell you anything about our wedding reception at all. No, the wonderfully uneventful reception in our event center was overshadowed by a visiting wedding party from hell.

Our reception was just winding down, and love was thick in the cool night air. It was the "asshole hour", and not one guest had turned into a pumpkin. The bride and groom had left with a trail of well wishes and blessings for a happy life. A few family members were gathering the gifts and mementos from the day. My team and I began to clean up and tear down.

While disassembling the evening's party, in walks a bridal party of about twenty people; the bride, the groom, their attendants and well-wishers dressed to honor the occasion. They bellied up to the bar laughing and joking that their reception had run out of booze. In all honesty, that should have been our first warning sign.

Our bartenders busied themselves taking orders. I walked up to the happy couple and congratulated them and let them all know that we would be closing in about an hour. "No problem," they all chimed. Excusing myself, I went back to join my team. Before the Borrowed Bridal Party could even drink a drop, all hell broke loose.

My monotonous task was interrupted by the mottled angry sounds of yelling and arguing. Too many voices to discern. Dropping my bag of dirty linens, I ran to the bar, where the bride and one of her partygoers were screaming at each other and one of the groomsmen and a dapper guest were in a shoving match. I headed towards the melee and ordered them to cut it out and get out. It was like I wasn't even there.

Someone grabbed the bride, pulling her away from the storm and I ordered my team members to call the police. When the police arrived, everyone was still pretty tuned up, yelling and occasionally shoving each other. The officers took the Dueling Dudes out of the bar and into the lobby to talk to them and see if they could figure out what was going on. When they did this, the rest of the Borrowed Bridal Party wanted to follow and add their two cents.

The gist of it was that the bride or someone called another someone's girlfriend a whore. I never liked the word "whore"; those were fighting words. I preferred the terms "free-spirited" or "morally-challenged".

By then there were about ten people in the lobby; me, four officers, including my superhero of a husband, the Dueling Dudes, and a few guests. The rest, including the bride and groom, had retreated into the bar. I was talking to my husband when the cops asked for the Dueling Dudes' IDs. One of them obliged with no problem, the other one wasn't going to do it, even after they warned him that if he didn't produce ID, they would take him in. This was the first time I saw drunk turn into stubborn and stupid; he wasn't going to do it. Half the guests were yelling at him to just give them his ID and the other half were yelling at him that he didn't have to do it. He chose his side poorly and suffered the consequence, as an officer grabbed him by his arm to arrest him.

The guy pulled away hard from the officer's grasp and when he did, he hit another officer in the face. I had never seen men move so fast and so hard. The other officers had him down on the floor and cuffed up in an instant. All the commotion garnered the attention of the other well-lit mouthy wedding guests. The ones in the lobby went after the cops and the ones in the bar rushed the doors to the lobby wanting to come to his defense. Quickly I closed the doors and one of my team members and I held them shut.

This would have worked better if we had already locked the back gate, but we hadn't. Off the Borrowed Bridal Party went, including the bride, veil, bouquet and all, out the gate and around to the front of the building, with drunken dreams of defending their friend.

The officers called for back-up, the guests were screaming at the cops, and the bride was fighting with the free-spirited, morally challenged whore. The police warned the Dueling Damsels to cut it out as well, and neither of them would listen. After the cops pulled them off each other for the second time, they cuffed them both and placed them under arrest. If you wish to incite a riot, cuff up a bride and put her in the back of a police car. Game on.

More cops showed up, the groom and his guests were putting hands on officers, some dumbass lady kept screaming for everyone's badge number, pepper ball guns were coming out of the trunks of the police cruisers to disperse the crowd, people were hanging their heads out of the windows at the hotel across the street to see what was going on, and I was outside on the front steps wondering, *What the hell happened to this beautiful night? Everything was just fucking fine twenty minutes ago.*

The "asshole" hour had not disappointed after all; it served up assholes, but they weren't even our assholes. It was bad enough when I had to deal with the "asshole hour" on my dime, but did I really have to borrow someone else's? Another hint here, folks, or reason for annulment: If your wedding photos include your bride's mugshot, just end it. Don't file the marriage license, just burn it and chalk it up to experience. Let it go.

CHAPTER 9

CALL ME A BITCH

(I'LL TAKE THAT AS A COMPLIMENT, THANK YOU VERY MUCH!)

Of the many things in my career that made me go *hmmmmm*, being called a "bitch" confounded and confused me the most. My kids had always told me—and in fact most people would tell you—that I am intimidating. I have never been able to reconcile this, as I am five foot nothing, overweight, a self-professed introvert unless in a business scenario, a mother of three, and a bespectacled grandmother of seven beautiful babies. Thinking about my own dear sweet grandma I wondered how I could possibly be intimidating?

When I asked my kids, they just looked at me like, really? They would tell me it was my presence, how I entered a room, how I carried myself. They said I could own a room full of people without even saying a word. I would look at them and say, "You mean like farting or what?" Their response would be an eye roll accompanied by an exhaled sigh of "God, Mom!"

One Christmas my team got me a baseball cap with the embroidered words "Neurotic Bitch". I wore it proudly when I was setting up for events, along with my "Chaos Coordinator t-shirt". In all honesty, people paid us for me to be just that anal about what I was doing for them. Occasionally, it meant I was the "bitch", so they didn't have to be.

I was the one, when setting up for an event, who walked the room making sure all the points of the napkins were to the edge of the table, that the fork was the same distance from the napkin as the knife on the other side. I was the one who would move a banquet table one foot to balance the room or improve traffic flow; I was the one to look down the line of chairs at the aisle to make sure they were straight. I would wrap and unwrap a bridal bouquet until it was perfect. In other words, neurotic bitch. No apologies here.

I offered no apology as I claimed this, meant to be insulting, moniker as a compliment, and as proven through the years, a necessary and "God-given" talent. This word was interchangeable with ambitious, determined, steadfast, tough, unwavering, depending on your age, gender and the circumstance. I used this talent to fiercely defend my children, my team and my customers. This trait did serve me well in certain aspects of my life and work.

The need to defend routinely shocked the hell out of me and

occasionally this trait or my hard-earned finely tuned training helped to serve this purpose. There were times I wished I had done more or done things differently. I tried, sometimes I won, sometimes I didn't. Situations would present themselves and there it was, the little warrior in my mind would be let loose, but other times people literally requested, instructed and paid me to be just that.... a bitch. Whether it was behind the scenes or out there for the world to see. All depended on the circumstance.

I was hired by a mom and dad to plan, coordinate and execute their only daughter's dream wedding. Devoted Dad was a well-known and respected professional in town and he was all in. Mom and daughter sat in the sales office on tufted couches where they relayed the wishes and dreams, they had planned for her wedding since the day she was born, complete with pictures and giddy, glowing excitement.

I presented the quote to Doting Dad and the Dreaming Duo and no one batted an eye or questioned an expense. They happily signed the contract and left the sales office, secure in the knowledge that the preparations had begun. You could hear the harps and cherubs singing.

Everything seemed fine as I did not hear from anyone, other than for scheduled payments and a few odds and ends for the next six months. Final head counts were in, flowers, cake, food, and spirits were ordered. DJ and photographer were booked, staff, officiant and rehearsal were scheduled. All the boxes had been checked. That was until Doting Dad stopped in my office a few weeks before the wedding.

I was a bit surprised to see that he was alone. He asked to see the final bill and the contract. I obliged confident he was there to make the last payment. Instead he told me to cut the fresh floral budget by a thousand dollars or better yet fifteen hundred if I could. Never wanting to embarrass a father trying to do his best for his daughter, but falling a little short, less expensive options started swirling around in my head, that would still give the Dreaming Duo their dream centerpieces on half the tables while easing dads wallet for the other half. Still a great option.

Before I could suggest anything, dad informed me that I could then use that money for a bar tab. I thought *"Okay that will make a nice cocktail hour for their one hundred and fifty guests"*. When he handed me a piece of paper, I quickly discovered that I had given Doting Dad to much credit. On that paper was a list of the names of people who would be allowed to use the tab: no wedding party, no family members. It was a short list of five of his cronies, politicians and business associates, period. I thought how noble, nothing like drowning your wife and daughter's dreams in spiritous swill for your closest buddies.

With that I kept my suggestions to myself and he left with my forced fake smile, my weak ass handshake and my faint hearted assurance of "I will see what I can do and I will give you a call." There was no way in hell I was going to be the one to tell the Dreaming Duo. God knows he didn't have the balls to do it, or we wouldn't be where we were so late in the game. Two days later I called him and let him know I tried, but it was too late to cancel or change any of the orders. He wasn't happy, protested profusely and profanely and finally hung up on me.

The night of the wedding, The Dreaming Duo were thrilled, and dad managed to still put up the bar tab for his buddies, but, thanks to me, not at the expense of his daughter's dreams. Dreaming Duo had the wedding they had hoped for, buddies were properly boozed, dad was a thousand dollars lighter but left with his image intact all the way around, except with me. I never looked at him quite the same again, but his daughter, wife and buddies did. I was the "bitch", but I was the "bitch" behind the scenes.

One of the most memorable Behind the Scenes bitch moments was at the wedding of a local pastor. He was a tall angular, anal Anglo man and he was marrying a beautiful sweet Hispanic woman. Throughout the wedding planning he was very proud of the sixteen-piece mariachi band that he had booked to play for their reception. They were a wonderful couple and their wedding went off without a hitch and was a beautiful affair. That was until dinner was served and the music started.

The mariachis were some of the best I had ever heard. Everyone's feet were tapping, and a number of guests had wandered back in from the bar with beers in hand, fully prepared to start the dancing and merriment. The Proper Pastor had other ideas and quickly pulled me aside. He informed me that there would be no dancing and no alcohol at his reception. Dumbfounded, I blurted out, "but you hired mariachis." More forcefully he repeated himself and informed me that I needed to make an announcement, over the mic, and tell the guests.

Not once during the planning did either one of them mention the "No Dancing, No Drinking" rule. If they had I would have helped them come up with an acceptable and polite plan to handle this delicate request. But now there was a room full of, two beers down guests, half of them Hispanic, listening to great dance music and he wanted me to tell them what? "Don't dance and no more alcohol?" Holy shit storm.

I refused to appear to be that big of a bitch to their guests. Proper Pastor was unequivocally and unapologetically informed that he was more than welcome to make that request himself, as I would not be doing that for him. (Even I had my bitch limit) He declined the microphone, and I retreated to the service hallway, request denied and mic in hand.

Everyone needs a trusted friend to be their back up "bitch-meter". You know that one person who when you are upset or are in defense mode will talk you down from sending that email or letter or leaving that voice mail, without either a drink first or a strong edit from a neutral party. Becki and I were each other's go to "bitch-meter" friends. And for this night I needed a little reassurance or a push.

With the sound of great music in the background, I called Becki to get her opinion of my declination of service. In all honesty his request hadn't met my "I won't do it" criteria. It was legal, moral and he had paid me. I recounted the story and asked for her honest opinion. I unfettered my mind when she agreed she wouldn't have done it either. Ahhhh, relief, my "bitch-meter" was in working order.

The school district in which we lived was notorious for not doing a damn thing about bullying. You know the "good old boy"; "we didn't see anything" bullshit that still goes on to this day in way too many schools. Our son, as well as several other students had garnered the attention of a persistent bully. The bully was a star athlete, on the honor roll and a boy scout. As the menacing of the Accomplished Bully progressed, we did all the things we were supposed to do; made a formal complaint, went to the school board, recorded the interactions, talked to the parents—and nothing worked. It culminated with the Accomplished Bully inflicting second degree burns on the neck of our son and another kid. All this during the week Accomplished Bully was inducted as an Eagle Scout. I never realized they had a badge for that shit.

The most that ever happened to thwart the little jackass was an inhouse suspension, because they didn't want to hurt his precious GPA. You would think we had lost, but karma was eventually served, although it took several years. One day, at the front desk, I was nonchalantly looking over the list of incoming arrivals, for the week, and what to my wonderous eyes should appear, but Accomplished Bully's name, with a note that the room was for his honeymoon. There was no way in hell I was hosting that little jackass at our hotel. Unfortunately, there is something called a walk policy that is an enforceable industry standard:

If you walk (move to another hotel) a guaranteed reservation, then you have to pay for the first night's stay at a comparable hotel, provide transportation and allow one phone call.

The only thing worse than letting Accomplished Bully stay at our hotel would be if I was forced to pay for his honeymoon night. I called my trusty GM hotline, and to their credit, they were empathetic and helpful. Who knew? I advised them that I wanted to cancel the reservation, told them the reason why, and asked if I had the right to refuse service with a guaranteed reservation without implementing the "walk policy". I believe that may have been the first time the consultant had been presented with that scenario, as I was promptly put on hold.

After a few anxious, elevator music filled minutes, they came back on the line and informed me that yes, I had the right to refuse service, yes, I could cancel the reservation, and no, the "walk policy" would not apply. The only condition was that I had to inform the guest. That I could do. I thanked them for the help and disconnected the call. Without even placing the phone back in its cradle I nervously dialed the number on the reservation.

A woman answered. I introduced myself and told her I was calling from the hotel. I let her know that the reservation for the following night for (insert name for Accomplished Bully) had been cancelled and they would have to find other accommodations. Surprised she told me she was his mother and that she didn't understand. I repeated myself. She asked, "Why?" Staying completely professional I told her that I had the right to refuse service and I was exercising that right and as a courtesy I was notifying them so they would have plenty of time to make other arrangements. She wanted to argue the point. To quell my growing angst and to quiet the bitch battling for free reign in my head, I wished her a good evening and hung up the phone. Round One.

It wasn't two minutes later when customer service called the hotel, stating they had the guest on the other line and were inquiring as to what was happening with their reservation. If you don't want other people to know, don't behave badly to begin with and don't try and act innocent and unknowing. The front desk clerk handed the phone to me. I said hello and repeated the story and added that I acted with the full support of the GM hotline. They thanked me and told me to have a nice evening. Round Two.

The next day, dad of Accomplished Bully called and wanted to speak with me and again asked why his son could not stay. He, his wife and son all knew full well what had happened between our sons and that his son had never taken any responsibility for his actions and never changed. I, to my credit, kept it professional and defaulted to the right to refuse service. While I had to listen to a few minutes of unproductive protest, he knew nothing was going to change my mind. Round Three for the win.

To Accomplished Bully's credit and, I like to think, to that of his new wife, he himself called me sometime after his wedding and took responsibility for his behavior and apologized for what he had done to my son. I figured everyone grows up sometime, even if it is forced by a sweet new wife or a bit by karma.

One of our properties held the dubious distinction of having the largest indoor pool and hot tub in town. Our modest town had a public pool, but it was only open when school was out for the summer. This made for a constant barrage of people feeling that our pool was there to use for free year-round public use. Contrary to public opinion we did not rent it out for parties as our insurance did not cover such uses. It was to be used by registered guests only; not by their grandkids, not by their aunts and uncles, brothers, sisters, nieces, nephews, first, second or third cousins or those that were just like family. I repeat, Registered Guests Only. This caused me great hardship over the years.

Like so many weekends I was at the hotel toiling away and noticed, through the two-way window in my office, people coming in through the front doors with birthday presents, balloons, coolers, pool toys and towels. Not very stealth, but all the easier for me. This was way more convenient than catching people with their asses half in and half out of the pool room windows, after the one dumb ass that rented a room had left it open and pushed out the screen. Or the ones that scaled the fountain or fences that separated the pool patios and doors from the parking lot. So, I was thankful for that.

Being the ever-vigilant general manager, I checked the security cameras and sure enough there were about twenty people in the pool area and a birthday party was going on. I asked my front desk team member if they were guests and she said she didn't know as they had been in the pool since she came on shift. I instructed her to go ask and to inform them that the pool was for guest use only.

She did just as I had instructed and found out that one couple was registered in a hotel room and the rest were not. She let them know that all non-registered guests would have to leave. They assured her they would, and she left. Fifteen minutes went by and, still no motivations to leave, so she went back and repeated her request. This time they turned a deaf ear to her all together. She came back to me and let me know they just simply ignored her and that they now had bottles of wine open and on the windowsills of the pool room.

Our pool rules were posted to the left of the pool entrance and clearly stated that the pool was for registered guests only and that glass was not allowed in the pool area. With this latest snub, my team member tapped out and it was my turn in the "bitch-ring". I left my desk and my work to go babysit the customers who thought the rules obviously and clearly did not apply to them.

Impatient and frustrated by their lack of cooperation and consideration, I entered the pool room and made a beeline to the group of adults milling around on the slick faux flagstone deck at the other side of the pool. I noticed no one had made a move to leave and there were four bottles of wine open on the windowsill next to the eight to ten adults standing around talking and drinking. Not being sure who the guests really were I directed my pleasant albeit stern request to all of them. "The pool is for registered guests only. All others need to leave, or you are more than welcome to rent additional rooms."

Quickly I surmised who the guests were as a wet, well

weighted, middle-aged woman was now pissed and told me to go talk to her husband and waved me towards a tall bearded man nearest the wine. I directed my request, instructions and options towards him. Despite the woman directing me to someone besides herself, Winey Woman chimed in and didn't think they should have to leave, it's not like anyone else was in the pool, and they weren't hurting anything or anyone.

I'm thinking *What the hell does that mean?* I didn't say that but did let the Winers know, "I understand, but just because someone isn't using their car doesn't mean you get to take it on a joyride and there is no harm no foul because you didn't wreck it and returned it with a full tank of gas." Among the rantings and loud protests of my "bitchiness" I again offered them their options; 1. Additional hotel rooms, 2. Leave and 3. The police. They chose option two, but not without filling my ears and mind with their colorful opinions regarding my behavior.

These Winers thought it was okay to steal services, to ignore repeated polite instructions and requests, decided of their own accord not to rent additional rooms, and chose to ignore the posted pool rules and staff, but I was the bitch. Hmmm? Tell me how that works again? Really someone, anyone tell me how that shit works? Since that Winey Incident I have been the recipient of more than one unfavorable customer comment recounting their fairytale version of, I was mistreated, without cause or provocation, on multiple third-party review sites. I was always the big bad bitch in the story. I could live with that.

CHAPTER 10

FEEDING FRENZY

(SUITE A$$! FOOD SERVICE)

While it seems like many of my experiences were in the hotel business, do not be disheartened, my food service friends. I had plenty of "what the hell?" moments in the food service industry as well. In fact, so many that, to this day, these customers are why I prefer, and always will prefer, to cook and do dishes in the back than wait on tables. Nope, too many circumstances to count.

Only four short years after the delightful experience of buying their mom-and-pop motel, our parents bought the stereotypical family diner across the highway. It had been built in 1953 and was the perfect mesh of small-town diner and rural truck stop. There were two holes through the expansive front windows from someone shooting off their .22 rifle and the restaurant only sat about sixty-five people total, but the dirt parking lots could hold thirty semi-trucks. Men would still ride their horses or mules up to it and tie them to the poles along the porch that ran along the west side of the building.

The booths were upholstered in well-worn light blue and pink leather and the color-coordinated turning post chairs at the coffee counter stood sentinel over the coffee maker, soda fountain and milk machine. The dessert case illuminated the day's cravings and the neon beer signs reminded all of the day's temptations.

In 2001 we replaced the little diner with a twenty thousand square foot restaurant, saloon, gift shop and convention center. The one small wood walk-in and single cook kitchen was replaced with a state-of-the-art, double line, six walk-in refrigerator kitchen. It was a huge change from quaint and quintessential diner to state-of-the-art. The only thing that went from the old to the new was our fabulous team members and customers, an old regulator clock, the salsa recipe, a ten-gallon hat and the beer can windchime made by a very special customer and our ghost, "Charlie".

Just as with the hotel there were the ones: Our regulars that we knew and loved. There was the Coffee Clutch made up of farmers and ranchers that would come in twice a day like clockwork. First time would be before the sun was up, around five a.m. and then again around two in the afternoon when it got too hot to be outside. They always sat at the same table, under their weathered, sweat-stained cowboy hats and ball caps, in the same chairs and drank the same thing, day in and day out. Strong coffee in the morning and fresh brewed iced tea in the afternoon.

We knew them by what they drove and by what they drank. We did really know their true names and more often their nicknames. There was Roach and Weasel, The Olsen Boys, Melvin, The Rons, Jim, Bobby, Bud, Terry, Gil, Gordon and Mitch, to name a few. They assured us over the years that they were all married, and truly we knew they were, but we would always tease them, saying we didn't believe it, as we never saw these fictitious females they spoke of and we weren't altogether sure that any woman in her right mind would have been desperate enough to marry any of them.

Only two things would alter their routine. One was if some outsider came in and chose that table to enjoy their meal, blissfully unaware of the imposition they had unintentionally imparted upon the Coffee Clutch. The men would sit somewhere else but send annoyed glances the way of the unaware intruders, hoping to make them uncomfortable enough to leave. Most of the time that failed.

The other thing was when one of them passed away. Their chair would be tipped towards the table, at rest, until after their funeral. No one would sit there out of respect. No one would speak of the loss—no one needed to; the tipped chair was enough.

Our regulars were an entertaining bunch and they had as much fun at our expense as we did at theirs. Barb, Karel, Pat and Annie were well seasoned, thick-skinned, natural-born waitresses. Karel was there when we first bought it, with her brunette barrel roll updo and hearty laugh.

Barb was hired by my mom shortly after she bought the place. The Clutch referred to her as the silver fox, due to her long, gently curling, silver hair. She wasn't that old, but her hair had been ripped out when she was dragged by a horse as a teen, and when it grew back, it came in white. Her heart was just as beautiful as her hair, and as far as I know, that amazing lady never sugar-coated a damn thing. Hell, none of them did.

She married her husband when she was just fifteen years old. They had to drive across state lines to do it. Her and Bob spent their wedding night under an overpass, cooking the duck he had killed for their dinner, because they weren't going to have any money until he got paid the next day.

He would be gone a lot, working large union construction jobs, and she raised their two kids in their neat-as-a-pin airstream trailer. She worked full time, raised kids and racehorses. She could carry as many as seven plates up one arm to a table and still have three glasses in the other hand, never skip a beat and deliver it all to the table hot and with a smile. She was a legend.

And she had to be damn good at her job, because she paid cash for two vehicles with just the coin she earned from her tips. She deposited her bills but saved her coin. Make no mistake, she was a hardworking, strong, beautiful lady and no one had better forget that.

One of our beloved Coffee Clutch—and I will leave the name

out—decided to test the waters. I am not too sure if this was completely his own thought or if some of the fellas might have put him up to it. Either way it would have been a theory better left untested. When Barb came to the table to refill coffees, he reached around and grabbed her denim-covered ass. Without missing a beat, the hot coffee and glass of ice water on the table hit his lap at the same time as she placed a well-deserved slap across his face.

He was embarrassed, mad as hell and all wet. He stormed out and didn't come back in for about a month. Either it took him that long to cool down or he figured Barb might have forgiven him by then. After that she never much liked that man, but by God, no one ever tried that again, not with any of the girls.

Annie was our cut-up. If there was a joke to be had she was the one to do it. When my husband and I were dating, one of my jobs was cooking over at the restaurant. His favorite pie was lemon meringue, so one day I decided to try my hand at making a couple homemade lemon meringue pies and I would take one to him and leave one for the restaurant.

They were beautiful, just perfect when I placed them in the oven. The meringues were light and glistening with perfect gently curling peaks. Karline, our lead cook, was proud of me. Hell, I was proud of myself. When the timer went off, I was so excited I took one out and ran it right over to his house, warm and golden right from the oven, leaving Karline to close up. Well, a few days went by and I never gave that second pie a thought, until Karline hollered at me. She was like a female endearing version of a drill sergeant.

Something was in the oven and it was keeping her from putting in two full baking sheets. I bent down to take a look and couldn't believe what I saw. It was my pie. Or rather, a beautifully peaked, shiny pewter version of my lemon meringue pie. It was now a charcoal briquette, through and through.

It had cured with multiple turns of the oven heating up, baking and then cooling down again, for dinner rolls, baked potatoes and other pies, for days. It had been pushed to the back of the oven with the first pan of rolls and so went unnoticed until it blocked the full use of the oven. It too was perfect, albeit black and shiny but perfect.

Annie used that pie for months. Every time someone ordered pie, she would bring it out and set it on the table. She would cover her mouth with her hand and start laughing. She served it to regulars and strangers alike.

One thing about Annie, she could take it as well as she dished it out. My husband was drinking a soda with my dad at the restaurant one hot Arizona afternoon, and Annie pulled up outside in her truck to come to work to start her shift. She came in and she asked them if they would look at her truck; it was getting hot on the way over from her house. (Keep in mind she only lived about two miles away. Thank God.)

Her keys in hand, my dad and husband headed outside to see what they could do. They popped the hood and prepared to investigate. What they saw floored and confounded them. They were just turning around to go have a much-needed conversation with Annie, when her husband, Richard, pulled up in a panic next to their truck. He jumped out of his car and ran over to where my flabbergasted husband and utterly confused dad were. He had been working on their radiator and in fact had taken it out to take it down to be repaired. He closed the hood with his tools under it, so they wouldn't get so hot in the Arizona sun, and left with the radiator.

Annie, not knowing this, jumped in the truck and headed to work. My husband, dad and Richard were all laughing like hell outside. All because they just couldn't believe it and Richard, because he was relieved, he didn't have a cracked head.

Sometimes it wasn't a matter of pulling a prank just a matter of keeping your mouth shut. The Coffee Clutch got up pretty early in the morning to attend to their morning chores while it was cool and then come in for their coffee. This morning Pat and Annie were on and saw the glow of familiar headlights as the Coffee Clutch started to arrive for their morning boost. One at a time they started filing in and the girls had their coffee ready, just how they liked it.

Now we knew they got up early, but you would think they would at least take a cursory glance in the mirror before they walked out the door even for chores. Either this one didn't, or he didn't have his glasses on when he did. His shirt was on inside out and backwards, with the tag resting just under the shadow of his chin. Do you think the girls told him? Hell no. Do you think the guys told him? Hell no. Do you think I told him when I came from the back? Hell no, again—after all, I might have been young, but I wasn't stupid, and I had by then learned a thing or two from those ladies.

Karel was the more serious of the bunch and if she reads this book, she is going to kill me. When Mom first bought the restaurant, the girls had to wear these black wrap-around skirts and peasant blouses. That was until the day Karel was walking between the service wall and the coffee counter with her hands full and that wrap around skirt got caught on the handle of the milk machine and promptly got ripped right off in front of the Coffee Clutch.

Oh my! She was embarrassed and angry, but mostly thankful she had chosen to wear a slip that day. The Coffee Clutch knew better than to laugh, as they might just end up wearing their breakfast. Thus, was born the new dress code: blue jeans and western shirts, thank you very much.

We had some characters that would just confound us, like "Gorgeous and Hunk". That is really what we called them. She was a large, curly-haired woman with a rear end you could have set a plate on. Never saw Gorgeous in anything but a Muumuu. Hunk was always in the same jeans, plaid shirt, suspenders and a gunny hat. Usually their grown son would accompany them and be dressed exactly like the dad, hat and all.

Now they came in at least twice a week and soon enough my mom instructed the ladies on what to do when they saw them coming. Everything had to be removed from their table and the surrounding tables and only given to them upon their request, and everything was to be accounted for before they left. You see, they would take everything that wasn't nailed down and put it in the mom's purse and take it with them. Salt and pepper shakers, silverware, ketchup, mustard, steak sauce, sugar packets and the container they were in, small plates, glasses and even the toilet paper in the bathrooms.

How did we know that last one you ask? That's because at the original mom and pop diner, the bathrooms were single occupancy and outside. That's right, I said outside. The locals knew where they were, so it didn't seem strange, but when travelers would come in and ask where the bathrooms were, we would tell them outside and around to the left. You think we told them we were aliens and they had to shit in the bushes or something, for the looks we would get.

Well, every time Gorgeous and Hunk came in, Gorgeous would go to the restrooms and then all the toilet paper—even the extra rolls and paper towel— would be gone. By the time she left, her giant purse would be full. It's like we were their trip to the dollar store. I bet they never bought ketchup, mustard, silverware, glasses or toilet paper in their lives.

My mom did have to step in one day when she saw their son lick the serving spoon on the lunch buffet and put it back in the food. I thought my mom was going to flip her shit. I was pretty proud of mom though when she grabbed the molested container of food and its' sad utensil off the buffet, walked it by their table and told them that would never happen again, explaining why it wouldn't and shouldn't to them all. They were no longer welcome to eat the buffet when they came in. They could only order off the menu. I mean, how sickening and unsanitary is that? It just gave us the willies and we hoped and prayed that this had been the first time he pulled that shit.

These women were great examples of how to deal with

people, good or bad. We had this little girl who worked for us, her name was Sammie, and she was married to Karline's son Alfred, who was abusive and an on-and-off drug addict. Well one night, while Sammie was on duty with Barb and me, he came in and wanted her to go home with him, right then. She told him she couldn't because she had to work. He said the place was empty and grabbed her arm. For a moment he thought better of it and walked outside. Barb asked her if she wanted to go. She said no; she was scared.

Barb put her to the inside of a booth and sat on the outside with me on the opposite side. It didn't take Alfred long to build up his misplaced courage and come back in, demanding his wife and threatening to beat her ass if she didn't go. Sammie and I were both pretty scared, but not Barb. She looked at him squarely and told him that if he wanted his wife, he was going to have to get past her, and that if he thought he was man enough to do that, go ahead. He wisely changed his mind and left. No one was going to threaten a woman, let alone put their hands on one while Barb was around. The marriage didn't last long.

In our wonderful little town was a great community college, where kids came from all over the country to go to school. Well four of these thirsty to be enlightened young women had come in to eat dinner. One of them ordered our signature special, my mom's meatloaf, mashed potatoes, vegetables and salad. Food came, and all the girls ate—all but one. She just picked at her food but didn't say anything when I asked if everything was okay and still was silent when I was refilling drinks, clearing plates and asking about dessert.

Just when I thought it okay to bring the check, the Meatloaf Girl didn't want to pay for her meal. I inquired as to why. She said she had ordered the meatloaf (like I had somehow forgotten what everyone had ordered since I was last at the table), and it didn't taste like her momma's. I stood there for a few moments and then, foolishly thinking I hadn't heard her correctly, said, "Excuse me?" Momma's Meatloaf opened her sweet innocent mouth again and said it didn't taste like her momma's meatloaf.

I told her I was sorry she didn't like it, if she had told me earlier in the evening, I could have had something else made for her. She became indignant and stated more firmly she was not paying for her meal. I told her that she was. She said she wasn't, thus the ultimate volley of *Yes you are*, and *No I'm not*, like out of a sleepy Saturday morning cartoon. Finally, I explained to her that unfortunately we did not have her momma in the back making her meatloaf, but my momma was in back and she made the meatloaf, and she was paying for it.

We ended up having to call the police and they verified that we really did not have her momma in the back cooking her meatloaf and nowhere on the menu, special sign or road sign did we lead her to believe that her momma was in our kitchen cooking. The officer noted that if she wanted food just like her momma made then she would have to make arrangements with her mother, as he did not believe that any restaurant in town had her momma in the kitchen, given she was from Georgia. Needless to say, Momma's Meatloaf paid her bill and walked off in a huff of misdirected youthful frustration and privilege.

I wish this type of naive bullshit attitude was just isolated to the youthfully inexperienced. But that would mean wishes do come true. Oops I forgot I do not own a pair of ruby slippers. Actually, I own quite a few pairs of red shoes but haven't found the pair yet that could make an evil witch disappear when I clicked the heals together. (Lord knows I have tried.)

Not long after we opened the new ten thousand square foot, Western-themed restaurant and saloon, I had the unfortunate pleasure of waiting tables on the bar side. I was less than thrilled, as the only thing I liked less than waiting tables was working the bar; I found I had virtually no patience for folks who couldn't hold their liquor. I am thankful that the great team I had always made me smile.

It had been a peaceful evening, with friendly happy customers playing pool and watching the game and I was in a good mood. My hopes for an uneventful evening, however, would soon be dashed. It was getting late, as we only served food until nine p.m. and the clock indicated it was already eight-thirty. It was my experience that not a whole lot of people sat down to start dinner after that. Yet, in walked a thirty-something very professional-looking couple with their "We only had one child, so we could have the experience" child that looked to be about four years old.

They paused at the open wood yucca-lined doors, kind of rolled their eyes and looked at each other like it might kill them to eat here. At their request they were seated for dinner in the lounge area and, to their credit, the child was perfectly behaved. I wish I could have said the same for his parents.

I brought them our dinner menu and a child's menu with crayons. They promptly pooh-poohed the children's menu and happily took the dinner menus and listened to the specials for the evening. After getting them their drinks, I asked if they were ready to order. For dinner they ordered our special, filet mignon medallions with Madeira wine sauce and wild rice. All three of them—one for each of the parents and one for their discerning four-year-old. I let them know that we had the usual children's fare, like personal pan pizzas, chicken fingers and fries, grilled cheese sandwich, and spaghetti. Nope, they assured me, their order was correct. The order was dutifully placed, and salads served.

When ready, the dinners were taken to the table. After bringing freshly refilled beverages to the table, I inquired about their food. The well-dressed and perfectly accessorized Helicopter Mom let me know that they loved theirs but that their child did not. I asked if there was something wrong with it. She said no, he just didn't like it and she wanted a new menu to order something else. I wanted to blurt out "I told you so", but I again kept my frenzied little bitch locked up in my justifiably cynical head and didn't allow her to come out my mouth to play.

This time I brought the children's menu, mistakenly thinking, lesson learned. Nope. I was the one who needed the lesson, as she again insisted on a regular menu for round two. Like a dutiful steward, I did as I was instructed. This time they ordered a Tuscan chicken Alfredo for the little tike. I thought this meal had a better chance, because even if he didn't eat the fresh mushrooms and broccoli, he probably would like the penne pasta, garlic cheesy bread and Alfredo sauce.

The second meal came out just as The Helicopters were finishing up, and Mom seemed peeved that it took so long. I let her know that the alfredo sauce was made fresh to order and that the entire dish was then baked. That seemed to placate her. Success! The child ate it, albeit only about an eighth of the dish, as it was a very large adult portion. Still, a win—or so I thought. When I presented their ticket, I brought along a couple of to-go boxes for the nearly complete leftover pasta and the uneaten medallions.

Mom looked at the ticket and wanted to know why I had charged them for three medallions. I said, "Because you ordered three." "Well," she replied, "my child didn't like it and we had to order him something else." I said that I was aware of this, but there wasn't anything wrong with the third medallion and they were welcome to take it home along with the pasta

Heli Mom promptly informed me that they didn't eat leftovers, so that did nothing for her. I apologized and offered to take the to-go containers. She snatched them from my hand and said they would take them back to the hotel for their dog and she was not paying for the third medallion. Keeping my composure, I let her know that we could not let our customers come in and order things off the menu until they found something they or their children liked and not pay for the options. Heli Mom paid but was pissed, and, big surprise, I got stiffed for a tip.

To me the real loser in this game was the child. What parent in their right mind 1) eats dinner at eight-thirty p.m.; 2) takes a four-year-old to eat in the bar; and 3) then orders them something like filet medallions with wine sauce? On what planet did Heli Mom live on, that she thought she could just have everything on the menu until she found what her helicopter child liked and not expect to pay for all the other stuff they ordered? Restaurants are not like an ice cream shop where you get a free taste until you find one you like or are in the mood for.

I truly believe that these customers are the real reason for the large walk-in refrigerators in restaurants. Screw food storage, it gives the front-of-the-house team members a place to go and kick and scream so no one hears them. A perfect place to go and let loose with, "F#@k off, f#@k off, f#@k off!"

After being through what I had been through growing up in a 24/7/365 family business I never wanted my kids to carry on this family tradition if they didn't want to. My husband wholeheartedly agreed with me. We wanted them to go to college, live life, experience other things, find their passion, find their dream. They always knew we would encourage them every step of the way: music, art, medicine, welding, machinery, entrepreneurship—if that was their dream, we were there. If that ended up being in the hospitality or food service, so be it, but this was not their nightmare or dream to live.

Marrying into or being born into our family should have

come with a warning label.

"People will judge you unfairly, they will call you spoiled and entitled. They will belittle your accomplishments; they will diminish your hard work. You will have to work twice as hard for half the recognition or respect. You will lose friends; you will gain false comrades. You will do good deeds, only to have them bite you in the ass. You will fight your cynicism; you will question your worth and mankind."

Our little brood had to have pretty thick skins when it came to the family business, right from the get-go. Our youngest daughter was no exception to that rule. Just like her big sister before her she started working as a hostess at the restaurant when she was just fourteen years old. She was good at her job and damn sure didn't deserve her first experience with the crazies.

One evening I discovered that discounted food and award-winning salsa, or the lack thereof, could completely unhinge a normally sane person. The busiest most hectic day to work at the restaurant was Taco Tuesdays. This was the day that we sold all-beef tacos and/or bean tostadas for just ninety-nine cents each. Your tacos came with chips and our award-winning fresh salsa, if you ate in. To go orders only included enough salsa for the tacos that were ordered. On those days we would go through twenty-five to thirty-five gallons of fresh salsa and sell over two thousand tacos.

Our team worked their asses off. It was well choreographed chaos but great fun, as the place was filled to the brim with people visiting and waiting in line for seats. If you ever want to see your team at their best, watch them when they are busy as hell. My team was like a well-oiled machine; they helped each other without asking, they knew each other's next moves. It was truly a glorious sight to see.

I guess I misjudged and was not fully prepared for how people would react without their chips and salsa to-go. I mean it was chips and salsa not the body of Christ. This bustling evening a woman, between the ages of forty-five and damn sure old enough to control herself, came in to pick up her to-go order. With a smile and a thank you, our beautiful, seventeen-year-old dark-haired daughter gave her the tacos and her salsa. Taco Lady asked where her chips and other salsa were. Our daughter recounted the policy but said she would go and ask the kitchen manager. The kitchen manager concurred, and she went out and informed her what the manager had said. Taco Lady instantly became unreasonably irate and started arguing and yelling.

Thank God there were other customers to witness this woman's behavior. Taco Lady became more and more aggressive, even as our daughter tried to stay calm, apologized and offered her chips and salsa for an additional charge. Finally, after being verbally abused for far too long, our daughter told her she needed to leave. Instead of leaving, Taco Lady hauled off and punched our daughter in the throat and then went for a second punch to the head.

Before she could land the second punch, our daughter pushed her away, with the woman stumbling backwards and falling into a cabinet in the lobby. Taco Lady quickly got up and ran out the front doors, tacos in hand. One of our team members called the police and our daughter went running out behind the lady to try and get a license plate number. Our daughter had to jump out of the path of this woman's car to avoid getting run over.

The distressed kitchen manager quickly called me and told me my daughter had been attacked by a customer. I was about ten minutes out and driving. So, I called my best friend, Becki, who was across the street, because she could get there before me, and I drove faster, not knowing the extent of the assault. My husband, who was on duty and had heard the call, was also en-route.

Let me tell you, it was Taco Lady's lucky day. Bolting was the best decision that woman ever made. I don't know if it would have gone well had she been there when my best friend or I got there. I know this though—it would have been a damn good thing the police were there.

With the plate number in hand, the police identified who she was and promptly drove to her house, where I am assuming, she was happily eating her tacos and salsa. Her next meal wouldn't be quite so tasty as they arrested her and charged her with assault.

A few weeks went by and we were called to a meeting with the prosecuting attorney regarding Taco Lady's charges and the plea deal, blah, blah blah. I walked in the small book-lined office and I could smell the defeat in the air. You could feel it like it was seeping out of the wood-covered walls and leather-bound books. The attorney sat there, subdued in his tailored blue suit and golden tie. He had a sigh on his lips and was sitting with what I would call a distressed, sunken posture. I was wondering why he looked so weak; we had a victim, we had eyewitnesses, it would be an open-and-shut case, slam dunk. Right? Wrong.

He informed us that Taco Lady's defense attorney had been in contact with him and somehow everything had gotten effed up and turned sideways. Okay, the effed-up part is my own translation. He did not actually say that. That's how I felt when he said an option was to drop all charges. It was all boo-hoo: she had been pushed into a cabinet and had an unknown previous back or spinal issue, which, they claimed, was aggravated by her being pushed into the cabinet.

I looked at that prosecuting attorney and said, "Really"? He said yes that she was claiming injury and her and her attorney were threatening—and fully prepared—to sue us if we pursued charges. I guess the fact that she threw the first blow, caused her own injury and was the one that committed a crime be damned.

I squared my shoulders and tried not to sound like the words were being spit out with the same venom and ferocity that was in my heart and mind. Trying to hold my now-shaking hands still, I confidently and as calmly as I could informed him that if Taco Lady and her spineless ass of an attorney wanted to play a game of competing unknown medical conditions, we would win.

His eyebrows raised, he leaned forward in his chair with

his pen at the ready. I informed him that our daughter had recently been diagnosed with a pituitary brain tumor and listed all the health issues that entails, and that she was supposed to avoid head trauma, which she was attempting to do when pushing Taco Lady away and trying to deflect the next punch. His demeanor did a quick one-eighty because now he had a counter to the sympathy factor defense and their sue-happy strategy. I now had a smiling, solidly squared, confident-looking attorney in front of me. With an iron clad case.

Taco Lady was subsequently convicted and received, I think, a year's probation for her assault. What pissed me off was that if we hadn't had that card to play, she would have tried and somehow made it our daughter's fault. We shouldn't have had to disclose her medical condition or use that card to even up the score.

Now, I agree our salsa is the bomb, but not enough to get arrested over, and who the hell attacks someone and has to take a plea deal over salsa? I don't give a damn how good it is—and our salsa was amazing—it's not worth your freedom.

It is funny what kind of behavior food and alcohol bring out in people. Actually, it isn't funny. For this book it's funny as shit, just not in real life while it's happening, but years later. Yep that shit is so ridiculous it is funny.

People have asked me on more occasions than I care to count, which type of weddings or events we had the most trouble with. They never came out and defined what they meant by "which", but it was understood and implied that they meant Mexican? White? Other? Never failed, they always assumed it would be the large Hispanic weddings. Not a good way to start off the relationship with your happily-and-proudly-married-for-decades-to-a-Hispanic-and-birthed-three-amazing-little-mixed-burritos wedding planner.

My response was always a resounding, bordering on irritated as shit, "No." I would, as politely as I could, inform them that actually it was routinely the weddings of little skinny white cowboys (i.e. the naked cowboys) I had the most trouble with. With that answer, they would get this incredulous look on their face and I would have a proud grin on mine.

This completely unnecessary conversation would always make me want to smack them for assuming a racist position, but I would choose instead to offer an explanation and attempt to enlighten them. Given I was privileged enough to marry into a Hispanic family, I felt I was versed enough to educate them as to the reason why.

I would tell them that it was the tradition of all Latino cultures to have great respect for your elders and your family, especially during important events. Meaning, a well-raised Hispanic person would never do anything to embarrass their families during something like a wedding. You would get the talk and the look from your mother, your tia, your grandmother, etc. If someone gets close to doing just that, the other family members will remove that person themselves and take care of the situation.

Proving my western wedding theory, we once hosted a rustically elegant western wedding reception. The happy couple and their guests had just arrived and everyone was preparing to sit down for dinner and finding relief from the heat and the highbrow clothes with a cold drink. The beautifully decorated ballroom was alive with the sounds of laughter and stories being retold to a new generation.

The father of the groom brought one of the bridesmaids into the bar and ordered drinks for him and her. He was dressed in his black western suit and pointed, polished cowboy boots. By now the tie had been loosened and he was ready to relax and have some fun, and I guess he didn't want any interference or rules to impede, deter or disrupt his path to merriment.

The bartender didn't ask him for ID, as he was obviously old enough, but he did ask for ID for the young bridesmaid on his arm. (As a side note, we always instructed the brides and wedding parties to make sure they brought their ID, as they may be carded.) Well holy crap, you would have thought the bartender had called the bridesmaid a whore or something.

The DAD (which now stands for Dumbass Dad), without warning or provocation, jumped over our bar like it was nothing, and started beating the hell out of our bartender. I mean, a full-on beat-down. It took five of the groomsmen to pull him off the poor guy. Needless to say, I came running, wondering what the hell was happening and thanking God that the bride, groom and most of their guests were in the ballroom, blissfully unaware of the science fiction-meets-fight club-meets old west scene in the bar.

When I got there, DAD was still agitated, flailing and struggling against the grip of the five strapping groomsmen restraining him. Since they had his little western ass contained, my first concern was my bartender who was bleeding from his nose and mouth. I asked him what he wanted to do. To the bartender's credit, he was way more lenient than I wanted to be and said that if DAD left, he didn't want to press charges. I went to the tuxedoed, cowboy-booted group and told the father of the groom that he needed to leave.

With that, DAD was fuming and went on a foul-mouthed rant about the bartender not needing to card the girl and that he shouldn't have disrespected him that way, blah, blah, whine, bitch, deflect, blah. I interrupted his colorful line of bullshit and expletives and told him he had only two choices: leave on his own or I would be forced to call the police and he would be arrested. Either way, he was going to miss the reception—one way with charges, one way without—choice was his. Needless to say, he left. At least he wasn't a complete jackass. Scratch that, yes, he was.

Even though I knew it had been the right thing to do, and I wouldn't have done anything different, a twinge of regret was creeping into my mind. There was a quiet corner in the bar, and I sat there, unable to keep from feeling kind of bad. I mean, for God's sake, they hadn't even finished dinner, cut the cake, done the toast or started the dance yet. I knew it wasn't my fault but there was still a DAD missing his son's wedding, jackass or not. My emotions were fighting with each other and it showed on my face, so I turned away while I reconciled the situation.

Just then, this quiet sun-worn little old man with the stereotypical full-curled white western mustache, bowed legs and weathered black cowboy hat, came up to me, put his arm around me and said, "Don't you worry sweetie, I should have shot that son of a bitch twenty years ago when I had the chance. I would have been out of prison by now and still at this wedding."

Alrighty then, I guess this whole situation was no big surprise. I breathed a sigh of relief and went on about the evening's duties, secure in the fact that the family was neither shocked nor disappointed by my decision. As the night wore on and I thought more and more about what the old man had said, I couldn't help but wonder, *Why didn't any of you people warn me about him or what might happen?* Nope, not even an inkling or hint of things to come. I mean, come on, let me know that there is an unreasonable belligerent violent jackass in the group. At least give me a fighting chance.

And, just for information's sake, when a bartender, server or whoever cuts you or your drunk-ass friend or family member off, or more politely, sugarcoats it by telling you it's probably time to "drink coffee" brings you something to eat, slows you down with water or says, "It may be time to call it a night", please pay attention and call it a night ,or slow your or their stupid ass down. Better yet, take them the hell home. Honest, we are not trying to be assholes or ruin your night. We really do want everyone to have a great time and still be safe. Damn, really, we do.

Just in case you're ever wondering if you or your friends are intoxicated, here are a few clues: If you end up in our service hallway, full of team members, and have dropped trou and are about to take a piss, you may be obviously intoxicated; if you are sleeping on the banquet table and using your purse or a pile of napkins as a pillow, you may be obviously intoxicated; if you walk past a perfectly wonderful working bathroom to go in the parking lot and squat your naked ass over the highway side of the parking curb to take a dump or piss, you might be obviously intoxicated; if you think you have the right to put hands on any team member or guest, you might be obviously intoxicated; if clothing is coming off, you might be obviously intoxicated; if you puke back up into your shot glass directly after taking a shot, you damn sure are obviously intoxicated.

Now if you think that the most important thing that happened to you on your wedding day is the fact that you can't take the remnants of a keg of beer that's left at the end of the reception, with you to share with your drunk, loud mouth, rude, dumbass groomsman instead of the fact that you just married the person you want to spend the rest of your life with; you are not just obviously intoxicated, you are an insensitive, misguided, complete and utter fool. (Yes, that actually did happen.)

During the planning of their day, this bride and groom were the sweetest couple. By all appearances, he was a very nice, polite and attentive groom, thus a lovely, loving young couple excited to embark on the rest of their lives. That is, until you mixed in a keg of beer and a Jackass Groomsman. His loud, drunk, stubborn, accusatory, stupid ass wanted to take the (maybe) eighth of a keg that was left with them after the reception, so they could finish it off at his house.

Unfortunately, that would be against liquor law as we did not have a resale license, only a bar/restaurant license, so it could only be consumed on-site. Fuck. You think I had pulled his mother's tit right out of his mouth or something.

Jackass Groomsman had a crowd gathered around the outdoor rock bar, including our lovely couple, yelling at me, calling me a bitch, and telling everyone I was just going to sell it to other customers, and so on and so on. Soon enough, the once Attentive Groom chimed in, angrily telling me, "You are ruining my fucking wedding day!" Blah, blah, *&#!, blah.

That was it. That had just worked me up over my last nerve, because you know who was standing right next to him? You guessed it, his beautiful bride, who seemed oblivious to the insult. I told him calmly and sternly but loud enough to rise above the rowdy, riled crowd that had been whipped up by Jackass Groomsman, "Young man, if the most important thing that happened to you today is that you can't go and slam this keg with your buddies versus the fact that you married this beautiful young woman next to you, with whom you have just pledged to spend the rest of your life, then you have bigger problems than the rest of this keg." BAM!

There it was, Light Bulb! Suddenly, there was an audible gasp from that beautiful, oblivious, innocent, little bride and she quickly pulled her groom away by the arm and guided him to the other side of the patio for a private conversation. This well-placed, well-timed, sobering comment also managed to shut up the Jackass Groomsman, and the crowd disbursed in shame without another foul word or drunken comment.

To his credit and the bride's, the Attentive Groom came over to me a few minutes later, shook my hand, thanked me for the wonderful reception and apologized for his previous bad behavior. I thought, *Way to go girl!* As for the big mouth Jackass Groomsman, screw you! I bet that beautiful little couple is still married to this day, and I seriously doubt the loudmouth obnoxious friend is still friends with the Attentive Groom.

When it comes to food and liquor, we rarely got the chance, in the realm of the hotel rooms, to exercise our creativity. Our team was instructed to always look at incoming reservations to see if there was any tidbit of information, we could use to make a guest's stay more enjoyable. If it said "honeymoon" or "anniversary", chocolates, rose petals and champagne were in order. If it said birthday, a cupcake. If it said funeral, late check-out of three p.m. These were all pretty standard expressions of our customer service.

On a few of these occasions we got to have a little more fun than normal, thanks mostly to guests who were willing to give us a morsel more than the mundane information when making their online reservation. Third party and franchise sites always give a guest a section for special requests or notes. I am telling you people, use them. It may not always work out this way but give it a shot.

With a spirited smirk on her face, my front desk supervisor brought a unique special request that would put a playful spin on an otherwise ordinary day. It stated that the guest would like a cocktail waiting for him at check-in. Oh yeah, this put a mischievous smile on my face and a plan in motion. My front desk supervisor and I were up for the task he had laid before us, and we excitedly accepted the challenge.

After all, it was our duty, as good stewards of customer service, to fulfill his request. We drove down to the local liquor store and picked up a travel-size bottle of whiskey, went back to the hotel and pulled out a can of soda from the vending machine and waited. We waited all day with our cup, can and miniature bottle of spirits, hoping and praying the guest would arrive while we were still there.

The day just dragged ass, time slowly ticking away, and us looking up every few minutes like we could will the hands of the clock to move faster. It was just torture getting all of our now seemingly boring work done, as we anxiously watched the security cameras every time the front doors opened, hoping it was Happy Hour. You would have thought it was freaking Christmas, for the anticipation.

Just when we were about to throw in the towel and leave for the night, there he was. Happy Hour had arrived. I swear we heard a trumpeting of angels when he walked through the door. As our team member started checking him in, Becki and I excitedly snuck around the corner and filled the cup with ice at the ice machine. I pulled out the bottle of whiskey and the can of soda and headed to the front desk.

Happy Hour hadn't noticed any of the unusual activity going on around him. He was busy listening to all the disclaimers we recited to our guests, at registration, before they were obliged to sign. That was, until we popped the top on the can of soda.

The telltale pop got his attention and it took him a moment to realize we were mixing him a drink. Yes, we did.

He started to laugh and said, "You've got to be kidding." We said no that we had read his special request and we took our customers' satisfaction very seriously. I couldn't help but ask him, as I handed him his cocktail, if he had ever requested this before. He said yes, every time, but no one had ever come through with it. They would notice it, but never did anything about it. He had been directed to the nearest bar or the lounge in the hotel, but no one had ever actually had one waiting for him at check-in. I really wanted to know, because if that shit worked all the time, I was going to make sure I communicated my love of Tequila on every future reservation I ever made.

He thanked us profusely and took his drink with him to his room. We were pretty damn proud of ourselves. It was kind of sad, though, to think we were the only ones who had done it. Come on people, how hard would it have been? All it took was thinking outside the box (or in that case, outside the boring fruit basket) just a little bit. Hell, for that one we didn't even have to think outside the box. Happy Hour handed us the possibility of a golden moment on a silver platter.

I did say this happened on more than one occasion. The second was the same scenario but with a female guest and a banana split. Again, no one else had ever gone the extra mile to do that for her either. It was so much fun to do, and our team would just light up when they found these little special request golden nuggets. Our entire team would be buzzing about it for days. You could feel the energy and excitement as they hoped they would find or be part of the next sugar-coated Service Warrior scenario. It was always a win-win situation—for our customers and our team.

CHAPTER 11

It's Not About the Money, and I Never!

(Of course it is, you lying fuck!)

Non-smoking. Hmm, do we all know what that means? Hell, my five-year-old granddaughter knows what that means. This is also not a new concept, nor is it rocket science, nuclear fission or brain surgery. Our registration cards thoroughly reiterated our non-smoking policy and stated that "If there is evidence of smoking by you or your guest/s, a two-hundred-dollar smoking fee will apply". This was signed by all guests at check-in, was on our websites and it was explained verbally upon presentation of the registration form at the desk during check-in. A little hard to miss and even harder to misunderstand.

I had discovered in my career that understanding or comprehension were mysteriously elusive concepts for the irate customer, regardless of the origin of their ire. My dad always told me, "If it is not in someone's best interest to understand you, they won't." I should have had that tattooed on my ass for as many times as that rang true.

Routinely, about once a year, paving companies came into town to seal and/or pave local parking lots and other surfaces. Due to the nature of their work, most of the time they requested exterior, casita rooms so they could leave their boots outside their rooms and such. Very thoughtful.

This paving crew was checking out, and one of their rooms had the smoking fee added on to their folio (For those of you not familiar, that would be the invoice.). Our diligent and conscientious head housekeeper had come to me with pictures of cigarette butts in cups in the room, the same in the waste cans, ashes on the nightstand and windowsill, and informed me that the room reeked of smoke. Pictures were taken, incident report filled out, room scheduled to be taken off market upon check-out for deep cleaning and, of course, the smoking fee added to the folio.

When the woman, a petite thirty-something, bursting out of her tank top, wearing blue jeans and work boots, came to check out, she saw the two-hundred-dollar charge on her folio and was furious. I guess not only was she the money person but the company spokesperson as well, and she was speaking up loud and clear, demanding the smoking fee be taken off, NOW! The more she insisted the louder she got. So loud, my front desk team member didn't even have to come get me.

I headed to the desk to see what the hell was going on. I rounded the corner and immediately tried to diffuse the situation. I introduced myself and asked what had happened. My team member showed me the folio and when I saw the room number, I knew what I might be in for. By now the woman was fuming and flipping her long black hair from side to side. I'd seen that hair flip thing before but usually it was with an agitated horse trying to swat away annoying flies.

The Paving Princess must have seen the recognition in my expression because she skipped the pleasantries and went right for the tirade, screaming at me that she wasn't going to pay a smoking fee, that she absolutely did not smoke in the room. I told her that we were not saying that she necessarily smoked in the room, only that someone had; possibly one of her guests. At the same time, I let her know we had taken pictures of the proof and had it verified by two supervisory team members.

Well, those explanations or justifications were an exercise in futility. I could've just sat there and not said a damn word and gotten the same result. Reasoning or explaining, as always, was not going to work. She told me it wasn't about the money, as she loudly assured me that she wiped her ass with fifty-dollar bills. She *did not* smoke in that room and she wasn't going to pay it. I let her know we had already charged it to her card and that it would remain as such. She yelled at me that I was the c-word (yes even my foul tongue has its limits) and a fat, ugly cow and that she graduated college, and that I was just doing this because I was prejudiced against gypsies. *What the* ....?

Patiently I listened to the Gypsy Paving Princess's out-of-control rant, putting up with being screeched at repeatedly that I was the c-word. She did have staying power and persistence; I gave her that. There seemed to be no end in sight. Unfortunately, I had work to do and I was quickly reaching my threshold for insults.

I told the Gypsy Paving Princess calmly and with perfect composure, that I respected her level of education and her financial position, and that I would appreciate, given her obvious expanded college-educated vocabulary, if she could find another word to use besides the c-word, as it was getting a bit redundant. I did manage to say that with just the slightest hint of a smile.

Well that just took the "pissed off bitch mode" to a defcon 4 level. I do believe she was more pissed about not being able to offend me or push me to lose my self-control. I, as a rule, refuse to get sucked into bullshit manipulation games. Same old same old, call the police, they rant, they leave threatening me or in a huff, prior to the police arriving.

How the hell could I have been prejudiced against gypsies? Can someone tell me how I am supposed to be able to tell a gypsy apart from anyone else? Is there something I don't know that I should? If there is, would it matter? Would it change the fact that the Gypsy Princess or her entourage smoked in that room? Hell, no to all of it.

During her tantrum I disconnected and started "why?"

thinking. *Why the hell didn't she just ask for a smoking room? Why didn't she just go outside? For God's sake, she was in an exterior casita room, she could've just gotten up off her lazy Paving Princess ass, opened the fucking door and taken a step outside and smoked on the covered porch? Why not just take four of those fifty-dollar bills she wiped her college educated ass with, and since she stayed a week, she had to have taken a shit at least four times during her stay, use the toilet paper included in the price of her room instead and pay her smoking fee?*

Becki had a real winner one day, and I was so proud of how she handled it. I wouldn't have changed a thing—that is, unless I could have clicked those mysterious ruby slippers together and sent the asshole customer home. This couple had checked in for two nights on a reservation to attend a funeral.

As a courtesy to guests staying for funerals, we extended a late check-out of three p.m. in case they wanted to change after the services, before they headed home. After all, we realized that during these times hotel rooms and such were unplanned-for expenses, so we tried to extend every courtesy.

After the first night and on their way to the services the next morning with all their luggage in tow, this couple wanted to go ahead and check out a day early. Becki, seeing that they were there for a funeral, asked them if they were sure they wanted to check out. She told them that we were full for the evening and that she wouldn't be able to guarantee them a room if they changed their mind later in the day. The husband took the luggage to the car and the wife insisted on checking out of the room. Becki did exactly what the guest asked and checked them out, handing her the receipt, thanking her for her stay, and wishing them safe travels.

The room was promptly cleaned as a check-out and immediately rented as predicted. Later that evening just before Becki was set to go home, who do you think walked back in the door and wanted her room back? Yep, Miss Insistent. Well, true to what Becki had told them in the morning, the room had been rented and she let her know that we were full and had nothing available.

The lady started arguing with her that their reservation had been for two nights and what did she mean she had rented their room? Becki apologized and reminded her that she had only done what she had asked and checked them out. Miss Insistent was now incensed that she was without a room or a leg to stand on.

Becki extended the courtesy of looking again for any cancellations or room moves she could possibly do to accommodate the guest, but there truly were no rooms at the inn. The lady was standing there seething, with her husband and luggage in tow. (Now if you have your luggage with you, obviously you did check out of your room. You didn't need to take all of that with you just to check your make up during the day.)

Miss Insistent just kept on berating Becki. In a grating and condescending voice, she told her she was incompetent, she was stupid, she was rude, and she was going to complain to corporate and get her fired. It just went on and on. Not that any of what she was saying would help Becki shit out another vacant room.

To her credit, Becki stayed calm through it all and maintained a pleasant look on her face. She extended more courtesy to Miss Insistent than she deserved, due to the reason for her stay. Miss was having none of it. She told Becki that she was going to jump over that counter and slap the smirk right off her face.

Becki was done. That was it. Miss Insistent had crossed the line and at that point Becki didn't give a shit what the reason was for her stay. Becki took her name tag off, slammed it down on the counter and told her, "Come on, let's go!"

We think Miss Insistent was shocked that Becki willingly accepted her challenge and was more than prepared to stand up and defend herself against her pointless self-inflicted tirade. She, her husband and their luggage promptly retreated to their car without another condescending, nasty, misdirected word.

Why do people feel the need to physically threaten and verbally abuse the people that could and do try to help them? It damn sure isn't going to support your position or get you what you want. It might cause you to get your ass kicked, arrested or, at the very least, thrown out. You never know the breaking point of the person you are directing your anger towards, and the worst kind of anger to direct at someone is the anger that you should rightfully be directing at the only person to blame for your predicament—yourself.

Some mouthy bitches, though, come wrapped in a much more refined package. One of our sweetest and most experienced front desk team members, Lea, checked in a well-dressed elderly couple for a three-night stay. The distinguished-looking gentleman seemed very attentive to his tall, slender, attractive wife and assisted her with her walker and all the luggage. She had a presence about her and her beautifully coiffed silver hair and manicured nails lent themselves to a kind of Cruella de Vile vibe. They were pleasant to each other and the attendant. Lea gave them their keys and the usual information, directed them to their room and thanked them for their patronage. Little did she know.

Strangely, they left their luggage on the luggage rack in the lobby and sat in the lobby just talking and drinking coffee. Not that unusual, except it was two hours before they eventually got up and went to their room. That's when the never-ending story, wait let me change that, the never-ending nightmare began. The calls just kept coming and coming and coming.

First call came in: Their television wasn't working. We promptly dispatched maintenance to assist. Maintenance went to their room and knocked repeatedly on their door, identifying himself each time. No one answered, so he used his key to open the door thinking maybe they had left for dinner or something.

That was his first mistake. Not that her husband was in the bathroom, but he could have been according to Cruella, and it was unprofessional of him to just barge in. He was informed however that since he was there, he might as well look at the television. He did, and it turned right on with the remote and worked beautifully. Before leaving he apologized to Cruella for the intrusion and promptly left the room without any acknowledgement or gratitude in his direction.

Second call to the desk: Their A/C wasn't working. Maintenance retraced his steps to their room. Again, no answer after repeated knocking. This time he wasn't sure if he should open the door or not, so he knocked a couple of more times and the husband finally answered the door and waved him in with an exaggerated sweep of his hand.

Maintenance went right away to look at the A/C and same thing; he pressed the "on" button and it magically hummed right to life. The wife, however, made a snarky comment while he was there, saying that he should have done his job well enough before they arrived so they wouldn't need to keep asking for his help. Maintenance excused himself and left the room, again without so much as a thank-you.

Third phone call to the desk: Their refrigerator was not working. Maintenance returned to their room, and this time the door was opened on the first knock. He quickly walked over to the refrigerator, just wanting to look at it, fix it if needed, and leave as soon as possible. It had been unplugged. Cruella went after him as soon as his back was turned to her. She maliciously told him he must not be very intelligent, or he wouldn't just be a maintenance man, but that he wasn't very good at that either, or they wouldn't have had to have called him this many times already.

With that, my proud and pushed to his limit maintenance man stood up, said the fridge was fixed, excused himself and left. To his credit, he held his tongue against the venom of hers. The Doting Husband never said a word to curtail his wife's treatment of the patient target of a man who had come to help them. Cruella had called just to be able to watch someone do those things for her and to belittle them while they did them.

The next morning the same sweet and now painfully aware Lea, who had checked in the not-so-lovely, Cruella de Vile and Doting Husband, was at the desk. Rounding out the main floor Service Warrior team was our friendly, fairly new, this is my first real job, breakfast attendant, who went to Lea for help. She told Lea there was an elderly couple still in the breakfast room, they had been in there for the last couple of hours, were no longer eating, and she was supposed to have closed the breakfast room an hour ago. The worried breakfast attendant said all she had left to do was vacuum, and she didn't want to do it while they were in there. Since the front desk attendant knew them from check-in, she said she would take care of it, thinking, no problem.

Lea went in the breakfast room and asked Cruella and Doting Husband if there was anything else, they needed, to which they both said no. She then invited them to sit in the lobby if they would like, as the breakfast attendant needed to vacuum, and she didn't want to disturb them. The lady looked at her and said, "Well isn't that just too bad? We're fine right here." She then turned towards her oblivious husband and started, once again, fawning over him, completely dismissing the front desk and breakfast attendant.

Lea turned around and walked back to the desk, not sure what to do. She sent the breakfast girl home and let her know she would vacuum after they left. The couple left about twenty leisurely minutes later, but not until after Cruella herself lectured Lea about customer service and her lack of skill in that department.

She never raised her voice, never cussed or used foul language towards Lea or any of our team members. Instead the warped skill and cruel presentation of words that were mercilessly wielded off Cruella's tongue were enough to make Lea and every other team member she encountered feel small and inadequate. Lea started crying, and Cruella just looked at her and moaned, "Oh boo-hoo" and walked away. During the rest of that day, Cruella ran our team ragged; "Get me this", "Bring me that", "Don't clean my room yet", "Clean my room now" and many more demands delivered with a demeaning tone and devoid of any gratitude or respect. They were exhausted, exasperated and never enough, according to this woman.

The next morning when I came in, I was informed of the behavior of Cruella de Vile and Doting Husband and that they were now in the breakfast room again and it was near closing time. I spoke with a number of our team members and they all recounted the same story, different circumstances, but the same resounding theme. In fact, my maintenance team was refusing to go to their room for one more thing. They were tired of being treated like shit. I thought to myself, *I cannot continue to let these people treat my team this way.* So off to the breakfast room I went, thinking I had a plan.

I noticed them right away and they were as described, a

very attractive, perfectly put together elderly couple, her with her walker parked next to her. She was indeed fawning over the seemingly unaware husband. I approached the table, introduced and identified myself, and inquired how their stay had been so far. She barely gave me a sideways glance and shooed me away with her well-manicured hand. Wow.

I tried again. I called them by name and let them know that I understood that there had been some unfortunate incidents during their stay. I again let them know that I was the general manager and if there was anything that they needed for the remainder of their stay to please not hesitate to ask me directly and I would make sure it was taken care of. My plan was that she probably wouldn't treat me the way she was treating my team, and all would be well. So very wrong; Cruella's tongue had no boundaries.

With an obviously and utterly bored glance in my direction, she asked, "So you are the general manager? Well goody for you. Isn't that just wonderful for you?" I must admit, I was temporarily at a loss for words. I had been cussed at, yelled at, lied to, even spit at, but never had I been treated in such a formally condescending manner. Now I understood what my team had put up with for the last forty-eight hours.

Well, they weren't going to put up with it for another minute, let alone another day, night and morning. I interrupted her one more time and let her know that, given the unfortunate circumstances during their stay and the fact that my number one priority was for all of our valued guests to be happy, that the only way I felt they truly could be, would be for them to stay somewhere else. She snapped that perfectly coiffed head of hair around and just looked at me blankly. Now it was her turn to be speechless. To my dismay that didn't last for long.

With an overly pitiful voice she asked me, "What? Has the staff been whining to you about me?" Not with real concern or inquiry, just disdain. I informed her that she had made one of our team members cry and that my maintenance crew was refusing to respond to her room anymore because of the way they were being treated. Cruella repeated what she had told my tearful front desk attendant: "Oh, boo-hoo."

After mustering every ounce of self-control I had, and in my best sugar-coated anger-suppressing voice, I let them know that they would truly be happier finding other accommodations, and if they weren't, at least my beleaguered team would be, and that I expected them to check out that morning instead of the next day. She just turned away from me and started fawning over Doting Oblivious Silent Whipped Had-to-Have-Married Her for Her Money Husband. I had begun to think maybe he was just deaf or possibly didn't speak English. I couldn't fathom that someone could, with full knowledge and understanding, be that accepting of the ill treatment of other people by choice.

I turned away, since I was readily being ignored, and stormed off to the front desk, posted their payment, checked them out and printed their folio. Just so there was no misunderstanding, I calmly and resolutely walked my chapped ass back into the breakfast room and handed her their folio. With a slight grin and a steely gaze, I let them know that I had printed it out as a convenience, so they would not have to waste time checking out at the desk. Cruella looked at me and said, "I hope you are happy; you seem to be getting a lot of pleasure out of this." I told her that nothing about this situation was making me happy.

With that, I turned and left. What I had really meant was, If I could slap the shit out of both of you, that might make me happy. If you get up off your bony ass and leave, I might be happy. If your husband would stand up and be a man, I might be happy. If you would just shut your mouth or grow a heart, I might be happy.

It took them an hour more to leave the breakfast room, and three more hours to check out. Check-out time was at noon and they did not leave until two p.m. Housekeeping had to go and knock on their door and let them know that check-out time had passed. They didn't leave. Finally, I had to call and do what I had had to do so many times before: threaten to call the police if they did not leave the room. Thirty minutes later, they were at least out of the hotel, languishing in the parking lot for another hour.

They did stop at the front desk before they walked out the doors and demanded that I come back to the hotel and explain myself, and that they were not leaving until I did. I don't think she thought I would come back. Hell yeah, I did. When I did, Cruella and Doting Husband were no longer at the desk. Rather, they were in the parking lot with her hanging on Doting Husband. I made sure I waved happily and said hello as I walked by—after all, no matter what, they were leaving.

For fifteen minutes I waited at the desk for one of them to come back in and demand a damn thing from me—which they didn't. I walked past them again as I left, this time wishing them a safe trip and a great day, with the best fuck-you smile you ever wanted to see and secretly flipping them off in the pockets of my slacks.

If the only way you can feel good about yourself or the only way your spouse doesn't direct that hatred toward you, is by demeaning or belittling other people, go to therapy. Don't just go, RUN! Get some help, take some classes, do something, you piece of shit. See I never or rarely cared what people directed towards me, I could deal with that. But you didn't dare do that to my team. I would stop you; I would defend them. I would do everything I could to make you happy, but I was smart enough to realize that sometimes meant that you would only be happy someplace else. And if you weren't, at least we would be.

One of the most frustrating things that happened over and over again was our defense against a customer's claim that we had overcharged their credit or debit card. We fielded at least four of these phone calls or inquiries from upset guests a week. They ranged from curious and polite to irrationally fuming and paranoid.

No matter how hard we tried to make sure the customer understood, they didn't, or maybe that would be better said as they wouldn't. I preferred that, as it lent itself to it being their choice, which I had unequivocally decided it was. These scenarios proved beyond a shadow of a doubt the previously stated mantra of my father: "If it is not in a person's best interest to understand you, they won't."

When you check into a hotel, your card is authorized for only the amount of your stay, plus tax and then a small amount is also authorized for possible incidentals. Incidentals would be phone calls, room service, damages, movies etc. Normally the incidental authorization is ten percent or less of a guest's entire stay. At check-out the final charges are processed against the authorization, and any additional authorization will fall off. Now, it won't fall off for one to seven days, depending on the bank and the card, but it will fall off. This is all spelled out on the registration card, but I swear no one read that shit or heard us explain it at check-in.

The worst thing that ever happened, aside from The Sign, was instant online banking. Before this, the customer never even saw the authorization versus the charge. It was something that just kind of happened behind the scenes, with only the final amount showing up on their bill. With real-time data, we were routinely lambasted for perceived overcharges.

They would bring us their phone or email us a redacted screenshot of their account data, sometimes within a half-hour of checking in or out. Not a statement, mind you, as the statement, when it was processed, took all of this into consideration and, just as in the not-so-long-ago good old days, would not show the once-hidden authorizations. To further our disdain for big business, the financial institutions had perpetuated this misery and did nothing to alleviate the stress and bullshit experienced by the first-string players.

Most of them showed the authorizations on the instant

banking sites as actual charges, and only when a customer actually called them and stayed on frustratingly endless hold waiting to speak to an actual person, would they inform them that yes it truly was, only an authorization. Yes, it was being held in lieu of the final charge, but it was, as we had by now explained for at least the fourth time, just an authorization.

Even with this, Instant Banking guests would stand at the desk, pushing their phones in our faces and wanting us to read their screens. They would tell us that they traveled all the time and all over the world and this never ever happened anywhere else. They blamed us for overdrawing their account, they blamed us for their NSF fees, as their check wasn't going to hit for two more days, and we already took the money out and shouldn't have. They wanted us to remove the charge or authorization. And on and on and on. Heck no, that sweet little authorization was the only way we were guaranteed to get paid.

Again, and again we would try to reason with them and repeatedly offered the valid, accurate and honest explanation that the funds were simply authorized; it was their bank that then would not let them access those funds. Oh, my Lord, they would call franchise, report us to the Better Business Bureau. They had even called the police. And each time we were proven to be right and had done everything just as we had stated, and it was all within hotel and banking industry standards.

Figure that each of the Instant Bankers took at least an hour from our day, four times a week and this has been available for, let's say, fifteen years. For fun, because, lord knows, it was, add in the additional time spent when they involved another organization we had to answer to. That means we had spent almost five thousand hours defending ourselves to instant banking institutions and stubborn paranoid guests. Five thousand hours—that is more than six months of my life, because some dumbass guest just refused to understand.

As a side note, sometimes that little ten percent over and above didn't begin to cover the incidental charge. One day, as I was going through the daily guest ledger charges in the computer systems, I stopped short when I saw an eight-hundred-and-forty-five-dollar phone charge. I thought, What the hell? I checked the phone systems and sure enough, the charge was there for a forty-two-minute call.

Naively I thought, *This has got to be a mistake*, and I called our carrier to ask them to verify the charges. They said the call had started there, went to California, then New York, then Thailand, and a couple other foreign countries. I was informed that the phone number was most likely that of a phone sex line. They went on that while, unfortunate and exorbitant, it was valid. Great.

I immediately tried to get additional authorization on the Fantasy Phone guest's card and couldn't; it declined. The guest information reflected a local address and a familiar, well-respected, God-fearing, church-going name. My front desk team member now on duty had also checked him in. She said he had given her this long sob story about his wife kicking him out and that they needed time apart to work on their marriage. No shit. I wonder why?

I called the room and asked him to come to the front desk, informing him that his card had declined for some additional charges to his room. He said he would be right there. I hung up the phone as I desperately hoped he would just bring me a valid card and we wouldn't have to delve into a discussion as to why. This would not be the case.

He demanded an explanation and verification of the charges. I was thinking, *Really, you're going to make me verify your deviant behavior.* I didn't know if he was that stupid or that perverted. Probably both. I did know one thing though, and that was exactly what he had been doing between 9:01 p.m. and 9:43 p.m. the night before, and that was way more than I needed to know. I let him speak with our carrier to verify the call and again asked for a valid card. He told me his wife had suspended his credit card for making phone sex calls. Thanks Einstein, like I needed to verify that or hadn't already come to that conclusion myself.

His explanation did nothing to help me get paid for his lapse in marital judgment. Fantasy Phone man just looked at me, shrugged his shoulders and said he had no other card or way to pay. Well, I damn sure wasn't about to fund Fantasy Phone Man's twisted version of the telephone game. I told him if he didn't produce a valid form of payment, I would have to call the police. He told me to go ahead, not thinking I really would. Well I did.

The officer arrived and I reluctantly met him outside, apprised him of the situation and gave him all the supporting documentation and sordid details. The officer looked at me and just shook his head and let out an incredulous little laugh. I had called the police for a lot of different things over the years; drugs, parties, drunk or violent guests, but this was a first for both of us. No one had ever called him, I was sure, and I had never called them to have someone pay for their obviously uncontrollable fetish. Who didn't love a challenge?

I truly believe Fantasy Phone thought that would be the end of it. But there was and is this obscure little law on the books against defrauding innkeepers. The officer went in the lobby and informed the "gentleman" of this little-known fact and let him know that if he did not pay, he would be going to jail, and the arrest record would become public information. Oops.

Well that just changed the whole game for him and it seemed for his phone call forsaken wife. While they needed to work on their marriage, the rest of the town didn't need to know the details. The scorned wife opened the purse strings, after a call from her husband, and he paid the bill in cash. He checked out and went back home, where I am sure the phone service had been cancelled.

And that is why you could never talk me out of the incidental authorization or guaranteed form of payment. Never.

CHAPTER 12

MOTHER NATURE

OR – WHAT THE HELL AM I SUPPOSED TO DO ABOUT THAT?

There is some shit I just did not and never would comprehend. One of them was why in the hell did people think that something that was completely out of our control was somehow our fault, and because of that we owed them something? It was just some of the dumbest shit I had ever heard. At least the liars and con artists were truly just trying to get something for nothing, and they knew they were lying; these next guests really believed they had been screwed by Mother Nature and it was somehow our fault.

I know that many times in this book I have reiterated that this all took place in rural, hot Arizona. What images does the word Arizona conjure up in your mind? Most people might say, desert, heat, cactus, etc. Well along with the deserts, the stunningly beautiful sunsets, the dangerous landscape and the stifling heat, we have critters that are quite unique to our climate. Things like rattlesnakes, lizards, scorpions, tarantulas and then, of course, the dumbass customer.

It made one wonder about a customer's level of common sense when they were traumatized and wanted their money back because, when they were loading their luggage into or out of their car or taking a walk around the grounds, they saw a scorpion. Now, granted, our native Arizonans had never been the ones to complain about this type of thing; they would just step on it or avoid it and move on. The non-natives, however, were another story.

You'd think they had just seen a goddamn yeti or something. They were freaking out and wanted you to go see it, up close and personal, and of course, it almost struck them, and they could have died. They for some reason thought that this sighting or placement of a scorpion was our fault.

Well, if I could have sprayed every inch of our property and down every hole on a daily basis, I would, however that was just a tad bit unrealistic and impractical. We lived among scorpions. True. They were abundant in the desert. True. Their sting is quite painful, and you can have a horrible reaction. True. The fact that you came in close proximity to one somewhere on the property being my fault. False.

If you think seeing a scorpion freaked these people the hell out, you should have seen the ones that encountered the occasional rattlesnake. It's accurate to say, and I will admit, that this was and always will be a pretty scary thing to do, even for the native Arizonan. That telltale sound could make your blood run cold. We generally gave them a wide berth, killed them with a shovel or shot them. If we weren't handy with a shovel, or didn't happen to have a gun on us, we called animal control or someone else to come get it and relocate it. Yes, catch and release. We were not heartless, and they usually didn't like us anymore than we liked them.

Rattlesnakes were not our fault. We would handle it after you hysterically informed us you saw one on the grounds, but I was not giving you a free room because you had the privilege of seeing one of these beautiful reptiles. Hell, people paid to see these in zoos. (Okay that would be behind glass, but still.) As a side note, I was also not going to take your camera and go take a picture of it for you. Honest to God, I was asked to do this. I declined the request based on; *You are a complete fucking idiot! That shit will kill you.* My customer service only went so far, and my own painful demise was a definite boundary.

You can kind of sympathize with the poisonous critters unnerving the guests, but the weather? I have told you about the hard and fast monsoon storms that were an annual and awing experience. They would dump huge amounts of water in a very short period of time, resulting in our infamous and dangerous flash floods. I can't count the number of times I had to explain the very large bridges over the "dry" riverbeds to guests. The monsoons were an impressive, oftentimes scary storm system to watch or be caught in. During these intimidating natural events we routinely lost utilities. Sometimes for hours at a time. People, this too was not our fault.

I have had guests scream at me, give me a lesson in how to creatively use expletives, complain to franchise, demand their money back and dispute their credit card charges based on "They failed to provide the goods or service as promised." Yep, you read that right.

One lady was pissed because she couldn't blow dry her hair in the morning. Understandable, but not my fault. Many bemoaned the fact that their alarm clock did not then go off at the appropriate time. I sympathize, but not my fault. Or they were pissed because their laptop or phone did not get fully charged, or their A/C or heater didn't work. Aggravating and uncomfortable, but not my fault. Innumerable complaints because they missed their favorite show or couldn't finish their work on their laptop. Regrettable, but not my fault. Better yet, their beer in the fridge got warm or all their food spoiled. I feel you, I sympathize with you, but I repeat: *NOT* my fault.

Now I know these people understood the utilities were out in the entire hotel or in fact out in a half-mile square radius or even the whole valley. They must have, because they were seemingly intelligent enough to use a blow dryer, operate a remote, use a laptop or go shopping. Yet they still were going completely ape shit over the fact that the power went out. Believe it or not, neither I nor any of my team members were at the back of the hotel turning on and off a giant damn electrical switch, laughing our asses off. Really... I swear we weren't.

"What exactly would you like me to do about that?" was my favorite way to respond to these Tantrums. It warmed my heart to genuinely ask them that sincere question and have them look at me for a minute with questioning eyes and mouth agape. They really had no clue what they wanted. Tantrums were just frustrated or pissed and felt they had the right to take it out on somebody. Giant newsflash, people: Just because you are frustrated or disappointed does not give you free reign to be a complete and pompous ass. One thing, just one thing I always wanted to know was what these entitled Tantrums did when the utilities went out in their own homes?

One of the biggest reasons folks travelled to Arizona was the sunshine. In fact, our valley laid claim to some of the sunniest and clearest skies in the world, thus the world's largest binocular telescope being located on top of our beloved ruggedly, majestic mountain. Both professional and amateur astronomers alike would travel to our blistering, beautiful valley from around the globe to explore the depths of the universe.

Now just because you came to Arizona for the sunshine and clear skies did not somehow guarantee that that is what you would get. When Mother Nature decided to blow in a torrential downpour, it was not my fault. On more than one occasion I received comments through both franchise and travel sites that Tantrums were unhappy because it had rained. Literally everything else on the review would be great, yet they would literally proclaim in writing that they would have given us a higher rating if it hadn't been raining.

Well what the hell did you want me to do about that? I am sorry you didn't get to count the stars. It pained me that you didn't get to go birding, hiking, or rockhounding like you had planned, but what the hell did that have to do with rating my hotel or service. None of the predetermined quality assurance questions they gave you to answer, asked you how the weather was. Surprisingly not a single franchise flag I worked under required me to guarantee the weather conditions during your stay. If I had control over something as big as that, I damn sure wouldn't have been working at any hotel and putting up with this kind of ignorant asinine bullshit.

It was bad enough that this shit was even allowed to affect our scores, but you would think there would have been a way, for the vexed and virtuous hotelier, through corporate franchise or the travel sites to dispute this shit and restore their hard earned, well deserved score, or at least not have it count against it. In reading Tantrums' reviews, you knew corporate customer experience bean counters read and realized these were complete bullshit, so how could it even be considered valid or relevant?

This was part of that "Life isn't fair", "You have to address the customer", "We want you to interact with them" CRAP! No really, this was just stupid and a complete waste of my, obviously-only-valuable-to-me, time. These should've been filtered out and not even allowed to be published. I mean, if they had an approval delay for our response, why didn't they use the approval delay for groundless, baseless, meritless Tantrum reviews, asinine, bullshit complaints and completely irrelevant comments that they obviously knew we had absolutely no fucking control over?

Occasionally you get to bear witness to an absolute freak of nature occurrence. A complete anomaly. Normally, October was full of fluctuating finicky tepid weather. The nights were just starting to provide welcome relief from the scorching heat of summer. The days were warm and balmy, having trapped some of the moisture from the now ended monsoons between the mountain ranges The cotton would be in full bloom, with its brambly tufts of white, waiting to be harvested, creating a captivating bed of white below painted skies. It was the perfect time of year.

A few years ago, during this perfect month, our town had the unfortunate privilege of being in the direct path of Mother Nature's powerful, unpredictable wrath. She unleashed a freak hailstorm on our valley, the likes of which had not been seen in more than one hundred years. Altogether, eighteen inches of hail hammered down within two hours. Streets, homes, schools and businesses were flooded. Car windshields were broken, roofs collapsed, townspeople were displaced and devastated. The Red Cross was dispatched to render aid. It really was a horrific storm. Our hotels and restaurant were not spared.

A testament to our townspeople, everyone helped each other. Neighbors helped neighbors; strangers helped strangers. To give you some understanding of the extent of the damage and the strength and fierceness of the storm, more than two thousand roofs were replaced in our valley because of Mother Nature's fury. At the hotels it destroyed our roofs, the screens on our windows and the exterior lights; the stucco was pounded off our building. Even though all of our properties stood well outside even a hundred-year flood plain; water flooded our stairwells, our laundry rooms, and our banquet and dining rooms. Despite our damage, we opened our doors to our friends and neighbors that needed shelter.

Many of the businesses in town had to close until the damages were assessed and repaired. Not us, never a hotel; we had guests and neighbors that needed to be taken care of. So, we were there, through most of the night and early the next morning trying to mitigate the damage, check in displaced residents, clean up and start repairing.

That next morning, I was in my office, still in the same clothes and without a shower. Thanks to the ever-present "Did You Forget Something" programs all hotels have I had at least brushed my teeth, combed my hair and had fresh deodorant. Team members were all accounted for and we knew that, while they had all suffered losses, they were okay. Everyone was exhausted and shaken. I was on the phone with the insurance companies—always a fun job—when my front desk attendant knocked on my office door. There was a customer who was upset and insisting to speak with me. I placed the irked adjuster on hold and went to the desk to see how I could help.

There stood a middle-aged man, nicely dressed in casual business attire. I introduced myself and shook his hand. A firm handshake like my father taught me. He wanted to know the name and phone number of our insurance company. I asked him what for. He told me to follow him outside and I obliged. When outside, he walked me to his car and showed me the hail damage. I am in no way a car person, but it was some type of beautiful little two-seater red sports car. Or it was. The car was now full of tiny little dents, like someone relentlessly beat it with a ball ping hammer. The windows were at least intact, so it was drivable.

As Ball Ping swept his arm across and away from his chest to accentuate the car, he again asked me for the name and number of my insurance company. I, in turn, asked him what for. He huffed under his breath and I swear stomped his foot when he threw both arms out wide towards his car, in obvious exasperation. I told him I was sorry, but our insurance would not cover the damage to his car. I explained the damage had been caused by an Act of God or Nature, whichever he preferred. Ball Ping was incredulous.

He proceeded to determinedly declare it was our fault. According to him we should have had covered parking and because we didn't, his car was damaged. I let him know that covered parking was not mandated by our franchise or the laws of our city or the State of Arizona. This would have been no different than if this storm had hit while he was driving on or parked on the side of the road.

I told him that while I sympathized with Ball Ping, this was in no way our fault. He told me that was bullshit and I would be hearing from his attorney and insurance company. I told him to go ahead and have them call me and gave him my card. Never heard from any of them, and you know why? Because both the lawyer and the insurance agent had taken a FINE PRINT class regarding Acts of God or Nature. I did manage, however, to waste a half-hour of my already-stretched-thin time.

Even freakier than the storm was the fact that we received three different customer complaints and comments regarding the displeasure of our guests because of the storm. I just wanted to bang my stressed out, pain-ridden head against the wall and scream. How big of an insensitive, self-absorbed, narcissistic ass could one be? People had lost their homes and livelihoods and yet Ball Ping and his fellow Tantrums somehow thought this was my fault and wanted a free room, their car fixed, and their whiny self-serving asses kissed? *Fuck off* didn't even begin to cover it.

Sometimes though, the interaction that amazed or amused me was not quite as dramatic as poisonous creatures or dark, rumbling storms, but rather something cute and sweet with the endearing undertones of a princess and her twittering little forest creatures. Like when, one spring afternoon, the phone rang at the front desk and my amazingly talented, well-trained and intelligent front desk attendant, KC, answered it. She knew it was one of her valued customers because a room number, from the second floor, popped up on her phone panel.

KC answered, eager to assist any way that she could: "Front desk. How may I help you?". Our valued guest asked if KC knew what kind of bird was perched outside of their window. For a moment she seriously contemplated the question, hoping for an answer. Then realized, *What the hell, I can't see out your window*. As suddenly as that commonsense thought popped into her head, she realized she didn't know what the hell to say, so there it was...awkward silence. The guest repeated their question, genuinely waiting for and wanting an answer.

What do you do? How do you answer the obviously absurd question? It was absurd because the guest must know you can't see out his window through the phone. Should you smart ass up and tell them there is only one bird in Arizona so it must be a roadrunner? Do you let the bitch out and respond with, "How the fuck should I know, I can't see out your window?"

No. KC just suppressed the reflex to laugh out loud, at least until she was telling us the story, and politely informed them she wasn't sure, but if they brought a picture to the desk, she might be able to figure it out. Happy customer. Albeit an idiot, but a happy idiot.

Please turn the page to enjoy Chapter 14 because one number is never used in the hotel business, and I am not tempting the hands of fate or superstition now. Thank you.

CHAPTER 14

POLITICS

(NO ONE GIVES A SHIT WHAT YOUR VIEW IS. REALLY.)

No, you didn't read it wrong, I did not write it wrong and the printer did not print it wrong. There is not Chapter 13, just like there is no thirteenth floor in a hotel or a room thirteen. Call me superstitious, don't care, why tempt fate?

If I have learned something in this industry it's, if you don't think you should discuss sex, well then you damn sure need to stay away from politics. Lord knows, the political arena nowadays is full of mudslinging conservatives and sometimes delusional liberals alike who don't want to respect anyone's views but their own. Everyone is so busy bitching, moaning and undermining, sadly nothing constructive really gets accomplished.

Our customers had the option of filling out a comment card and either leaving it at the front desk or in their room. These would be gathered from the front desk or maid's cart and put in my box to be read. I was going over them one morning to see if there were any issues we needed to address; maybe a team member's service we could recognize, or anything we could use for training purposes, when one piqued my interest.

A man not only filled out the entire card but used most of the back as well. He let us know that he did not appreciate us trying to shove our political agenda down his throat with his breakfast. Concerned Citizen wrote that he knew who we voted for. He continued that he hadn't even had the chance to finish his breakfast because he lost his appetite listening to the fake news, Republican conservative agenda of the major news channel we had playing in our breakfast room. He said we probably just supported this station and its position because we too were greedy, pushy businesspeople just like the President. We were notified that he would not be staying with us in the future, as his conscience would not let him. Concerned Citizen informed me that we should learn to keep politics out of our business. Wow, who pissed in his cereal bowl? Or corn flakes, if it is more politically correct.

No agenda-pushing here. Franchise dictated that we provide a television in the breakfast room. This would generally be tuned to a news station, sometimes national, sometimes local. The one thing the franchise nor I ever mandated was what channel the televisions had to be on, only that they were to be on some news or weather channel or something similar for our guests. No agenda, just background noise. If Concerned Citizen had bothered to ask to have it turned to another nationally recognized news station, the breakfast attendant would have obliged, just like we would if families were in and they requested to watch cartoons or a family channel.

It was not brain surgery, he just needed to ask. If he could open his hard-lined mouth or sharpen his pencil to bitch, then why not simply open his mouth and tell us what he would like? Thus, he would have simply solved his own freaking problem. Instead the privileged, safe-space ass just assumed he knew who we were and our motivation. I immediately thought, *Not fair, you self-righteous prick. Learn to use your words and stop creating your own nightmare.*

By the way, at the writing of this book, Concerned Citizen was still staying with us on a regular basis and was still routinely bitching about us providing the free copies of the *USA Today* newspaper. To him it was obviously a plot of ours to push a covert agenda on our customers. Sad to disappoint the conspiracy theorists out there, but it wasn't. Nothing quite so sinister afoot, just one of the many franchise mandates. We were required to provide a free daily newspaper to our guests. Period. Do you honestly think our small town produced a daily newspaper? Hell no.

This left our only franchise-acceptable and readily available option as *USA Today*. That's it. End of story. I swear though, I would have liked to have screwed with him just a little bit. You know, maybe a stack of politically incorrect bumper stickers on the counter or a roll of elephant-laden toilet paper in his bathroom. Better yet, the subtle placement of GOP stickers on each of the devil's newspapers. That would have been completely unprofessional, a little mean and deeply satisfying. Probably would have pushed him over the edge, but really, I think Concerned Citizen was pretty much teetering there anyway.

Speaking of self-righteous, our valley is privileged to be home to a Mormon temple. No, I am not Mormon nor am I prejudiced against Mormons. It's a beautiful building and we are proud to have one in our valley, regardless if I am allowed in it or not. Because of this, wonderfully modest and some self-proclaimed morally superior families came for weddings or to do temple work. A nice wholesome reason to travel to our valley.

In the lobby of one of our hotels, the owners displayed several pieces of their own personal artwork, sculptures, paintings and such. One of the statues was by a well-known artist who had also been a personal friend of theirs. The dark bronze statue depicted a nude Native American woman walking thigh-deep in water with the wind blowing through her hair. The statue was beautifully and tastefully done, and it sat on a small side table next to the baby grand piano.

The passionate author of this comment card was also very prolific and needed more space than what the front of the card would allow. The Passionate Prude was incensed that we had a nude statue in our lobby. It should not be displayed, and it was egregiously our fault that wholesome men and women were forced to look at such vulgarity.

She found the piece to be pornographic and offensive. The Passionate Prude informed us that she was up here to do work in the temple and that piece was contrary to all she believed in. (I figured she just didn't like sculptures.) She went on to demand its immediate removal. If we did not comply, neither her nor her temple worthy husband would be staying with us again. Hmm, I had to think about that a minute.

The statue had been on display for fifteen years and we had never received a single complaint, rather a number of compliments on the beauty and artistry of the piece. I carefully and thoughtfully weighed my options. Beautiful statue-uptight woman, fifteen years-one-night, God-given talent on display-manmade prejudice. Statue is still in the lobby—I don't think the Passionate Prude, or her husband ever stayed again.

In Arizona it was and is against the law to have a firearm inside an establishment that served alcohol. By law, signs that reflected that applicable statute had to be displayed at or near the entrance. The same law applied to bars as well as restaurants that served alcohol. Simple enough.

One day I received a phone call from a gentleman who wanted to host a luncheon for twenty-five to forty people. Not a problem. I proceeded to get some additional information, such as date, time and menu. We spent about ten minutes on the phone, and I assured him we would have everything ready for him and his party when they arrived. Right before we ended the call, he told me that everyone would be open carrying. For those of you who don't know what that means, they would all have a loaded gun on them in plain sight.

Well doesn't that just paint a rosy damn picture. I politely informed Open Carry that I could not knowingly allow that. With misplaced and insincere shock and anger, he asked, "What?" I repeated myself and let him know that by law I could not, thus would not knowingly allow anyone but uniformed law enforcement, to open carry in the restaurant, because we had a liquor license.

He proceeded to tell me that I was un-American, that it was their constitutional right to carry guns, that we were just a bunch of liberals, and on and on and blah, blah, blah. I kind of stopped listening after the un-American bullshit or I was so pissed off by then that all the blood had rushed to my head and blocked off my ears.

Before he could continue his well-planned overzealous rant, I not so politely informed Open Carry that we had flown an American flag at every business we had ever had. I told him that my grandfather spent fourteen years in a VA hospital before he could come home. I told him that beautiful flag draped his coffin at his funeral and it now sits at my father's house in a place of honor. I told him we had "One Nation Under God" and "In God We Trust" in twenty-inch-high letters on the walls of our restaurant. I told him he didn't have the right to call anyone un-American until he knew their story. I told him he was lucky to live in a free county where; men and women better than him had sacrificed for his right to bear arms. I informed him that if they had just come in with their guns concealed carry no one would have known, and they could have enjoyed their meal. I told him our beloved Constitution guaranteed his right to bear arms and that it didn't say shit about how a state could or could not allow them to carry said arms. Click.

You can call me a lot of things and people have. Bitch, cunt, stupid, whatever, but don't you dare ever call me un-American. I *WILL* defend that shit. We do not have to agree with each other, hell we don't even have to like each other, but by God we need to respect each other and realize there is one thing we all have in common, regardless of our differences: We are Americans and should be damn proud of it. (If you aren't proud of it, and you aren't doing something constructive to change what you don't like, then get the hell out.)

Okay, rant over. I truly had to walk away for a minute. Just remembering that interaction pissed me off. Yeah, yeah, I know, no one else is in control of your emotions but you. Blah, blah, blah. You are absolutely correct, and I choose to let that piss me off, because some things just should.

Guns are a big thing in Arizona. We can open carry and I don't know anyone here who doesn't own a gun. My husband, besides being an officer, was also the firearms instructor for his department. We taught our children from a young age how to safely handle any gun, loaded or not, and that they should always assume that any gun is loaded, and it was to be handled as such. He taught them how to shoot and shoot well, and they all do.

Needless to say, we enjoyed guns and shooting. But again, I stress that safety was always our first priority. Our guns were either on our person or locked in a gun safe. An actual safe, not one of those glass covered invitations to an intruder to then become armed, display cases. And we always carried when we travelled.

Well, so do a lot of other people, but they either didn't have the same level of respect or were plain oblivious, I guess, to the dangers of loaded weapons. Remember how I said if we were wrong, we would fix it or take care of it? Well this time we weren't wrong, but I comped the room because it was just the right thing to do.

We checked a nice family of five into a hotel room. They were travelling through and were there for just one night. When I left for home, they were happily enjoying relief from the heat in the outdoor pool. About an hour later I was cooking dinner and got a frantic call from my front desk attendant that this family had found a loaded gun in their room.

I didn't even ask for more details. I said I'd be right there, hung up the phone, turned off the stove and jumped in my car and headed to town. The wheels in my head were turning damn near as fast as the ones on my car, wondering the whole way there how the housekeeper and inspector missed it. How could this possibly have happened? I should have known there would be more to the story.

When I arrived and nearly sprinted through the office doors, the mother was leaning on the front desk counter and was duly upset. I assured her she had every right to be. I apologized and said I didn't know how housekeeping and the inspector missed this, as it was our policy to leave all drawers open until the room had been inspected, ensuring that any item left behind by a previous guest would be found and processed.

Then she told me how it happened. After swimming, they were getting the kids ready for bed. Her eight-year-old son had just finished taking a shower and pulled down the towel that was folded and sitting on the towel rack. It was the bottom towel, as one of the other kids had used the top one before him. When he did this, a gun fell out and hit the tiled floor. Her husband heard the impact and the startled yelp from their son and ran to the bathroom.

The little boy, scared by the whole thing, had run out of the bathroom door, wrapping the towel around him. The dad, through the now-open door, saw the gun on the wet bathroom floor. He grabbed the gun and discovered it was loaded. They brought it to the desk and were visibly shaken. This could have been so much worse. That gun could have misfired when it hit the floor, or one of the kids could have found it and innocently pulled the trigger and hurt or killed themselves or someone else.

It was the trailer to every parent's worst nightmare. By the grace of God, it didn't misfire, and dad got ahold of it before one of the kids did. Thanking the good lord above it hadn't become a horrible tragedy, I comped their room. It was the very least I could do. We called the police and gave them the gun so they could run the numbers. After all, who forgets their loaded weapon and doesn't come back for it or call? The last time the room was rented was three days prior. Plenty of time to realize it was missing.

The reservation was from out-of-state and had been made

through a third-party booking site. The police never found the owner. Did someone truly forget it, or did someone just ditch a weapon that was used to commit a crime or had been stolen? We would never know and were just thankful no one was physically hurt. To whoever left that gun, I hope you read this, you asshole. Way to unsuccessfully make an argument for Second Amendment rights, jackass.

Now you should have seen the inside of our restaurant. It was full of mounts—you know, taxidermy animal heads: Buffalo, moose, deer, elk, antelope, javelina, big horn sheep, black bear, even some fish and a jackalope. They were an impressive sight among the antiques, rustic wagons, and memorabilia that covered the walls of the restaurant and saloon, telling the story of the rugged west. There had to be at least twenty-five or so, and they were kind of hard to miss. No matter which way you came in or where you sat, a mount would be in your direct line of sight.

This very nice young lady came in to eat lunch one day and decided to fill out an application for a job while she was there. Her paperwork went to HR and moved through the usual processing before landing on my desk. She was called in for an interview. Just before she was set to arrive for the appointment, I got a phone call. It was her. I naively thought she might have been calling to tell me she had been delayed and immediately gave her extra points for thoughtfulness.

My brownie point bliss was short-lived when she explained that she just couldn't come in for the interview. She let me know that she had eaten lunch there the day she had applied, and she could hardly get through it because of all the dead animal heads. They scared her, and she couldn't help but wonder what kind of people we were, given we decorated our restaurant with the heads of dead animals. I thanked her and hung up the phone, not even attempting an explanation or justification.

In retrospect, what I should have told her was that really, no animals were harmed in the creation of the mounts and assure her that all of the animals had died of natural causes. In all honesty, not too far from the truth, all but eight of the mounts were purchased, so not positive where they ultimately came from, and the others were killed by the owners or someone they knew, and they did not die in vain.

Their meat was indeed eaten. And if she was so damn uncomfortable, why did she turn in the application? I mean, what? Did she think they would just magically come back to life and prance out the door with the garden gnomes and blue birds or we would have suddenly had a vegan epiphany and taken them down in solidarity with her? Uh, no and not sorry to disappoint.

I could go on, but this book is supposed to be funny, dammit.

CHAPTER 15

DRUGS AND BOOZE

.

(NO FURTHER EXPLANATION NEEDED.)

How could I have chapters on sex and politics and not have one on drugs and booze? That would just be silly. Oh, and if you count the rap groups, we might account for the rock and roll portion too.

Just like the hard-working parents who raised me, the vast majority of our customers were also cut from the same cloth of hard-working, responsible, dedicated people. My parents didn't drink and raised their kids not to as well—a futile endeavor. The town was split on the consumption of extracurricular spiritous beverages. There were the Mormons, or at least the good ones that did not partake, God forbid. Then there were the Catholics, who did, because there was nothing wrong with a little wine or cerveza—after all, God did. There was a third class: the Mormons who drank but didn't want anyone to know they did. Everyone else just fell somewhere in between.

This third class wouldn't be caught dead in a bar or with a beer on their table in public. No, these fine, upstanding citizens would cruise the dusty canal roads, checking their fields with their like-minded secretly rebellious friends, neighbors, cousins or brothers, slamming back a six pack and tossing the cans out the window into their truck beds, like clandestine, carefree teenagers. I would have added here "with the wind blowing through their hair", but none of them had enough hair under their cowboy hats to blow through. Evidence, you say. Heck no, for all their wives knew they were doing their part for the environment, picking up cans tossed out by irresponsible drunkards. Bless their souls.

I myself, given the stress of being a serial entrepreneur, damn sure deserved to be an alcoholic. Should have been an alcoholic. But no. I did, however, develop a penchant for the occasional taste of truly good Tequila and the training wheels be damned. I liked sipping a shot just poured over ice. If you need salt, lime, lemon, tabasco or margarita mix to enjoy Tequila, you are drinking the wrong Tequila, my friend.

Others, I learned, needed a little extra help to get through their day. Something more than faith, family, friends, food or even the forbidden, frowned-upon, fermented fare. They needed a chemically or horticulturally induced form of exaltation or relaxation.

More often than not, I would work throughout my day in a state of sweet oblivion, naively and blissfully unaware that anything involving the dark side was going on, until a very serious-looking officer was standing at my desk. This was probably the worst way to discover that something was amiss at any property. This time would be no different.

My team member knocked lightly on my door and nonchalantly informed me there were a couple of humorless police officers wanting to talk to me. Wasn't shocked, offended or concerned by what I thought was a misrepresentation of their demeanor. Most officers have a guarded serious look about them. The longer they serve, the more stoic the look.

At first, I wasn't too alarmed to hear it, given my husband's profession. Sometimes officers stopped by for coffee in the lobby or they might ask for me to make them a reservation for incoming family. Rounding the corner, I noticed the look on their faces was all business. Their feet were apart in a solid, purposeful stance and their hands were resting squarely on their heavy black duty belts. Seeing their faces, my smile faded as I approached the counter, instinctively knowing this was not going to be a friendly visit over coffee. I steeled myself for whatever was coming.

They informed me they had stopped a vehicle on its way into town for a routine traffic violation and, during the search of the truck, they discovered the makings of a meth lab in the truck bed. And yes, it was my lucky day, as the unfortunate motorist stated he was on his way to our hotel to meet up with friends. The friends had gotten him a job with one of the big contractors for the mine. The officers were concerned that the guests in question might have a meth lab already set up in our hotel room. Oh Christ, I wasn't prepared in the slightest for that.

They gave me the room number, I gave them all the information I had, including the housekeeping logs that showed they had been a DND, or do not disturb room, since they arrived. They had a search warrant; I had a master key. There were no niceties, no joking, just direct questions and complete answers.

Before they left for the room, they had me check to make sure the rooms around the one in question were vacant and that no guests or team members were in the near vicinity, other than those possibly involved in the illegal activity. I was quickly schooled in the nuances of a meth lab. Mainly, that if not handled correctly they can explode like a giant bomb. The officers proceeded to the room. Me, I gladly stayed at the desk, nervously pacing and awaiting the outcome.

The officers entered the room and, lo and behold, there were two people sleeping in the beds. The room was a mess and the rest of what they would have needed to start a meth lab was there and waiting for the Unfortunate Motorist. The two parties were each bringing their pieces to our hotel, to put their puzzle together and get a meth lab up and running.

These Meth Heads were from Tennessee; had flown here for work, had good jobs, and this is what they needed to do on the side? I am all for working a second job or getting a little side hustle on to make ends meet, but a meth lab? Christ. Really?

I get it, sometimes the days between paydays are long or special expenses arise. This I knew too well. When my oldest daughter was getting married, I studied for my tax specialist certification with a nation-wide tax accounting service and did taxes all one season to help pay for the wedding, and my husband worked a second job. Besides the extra pay and whole different set of stories, I had the privilege of nailing another piece of paper to my wall. I get it.

The police took care of the Meth Heads from then on and strongly suggested to us that even though the meth lab had not yet been completely assembled, that we should contact an appropriate hazmat team to process the room. I was like "Hazmat?" What the hell did they mean, "Hazmat"? I had no clue but would soon be well schooled.

Oh, what a glorious new experience for me. They did not teach anyone how to deal with this shit in hospitality management school or any Kumbaya customer service training seminar I had ever fucking attended. Thank God the officers just happened to have the name and number of a trusted and reliable company that specialized in this sort of thing.

It didn't hit me until later: I only had to be given this number for hopefully a one-time event; those poor bastards carried it around with them like I'd carry a freaking pen. They dealt with a much more unique and challenging type of clientele and had a much more interesting set of numbers in their rolodex.

I contacted the company these Meth Heads worked for, as they were paying for their room, and I reluctantly contacted the hazmat team. The hazmat remediation company arrived and said the test to see if the room needed to be decontaminated would cost fifteen hundred dollars and that if meth had ever even been smoked in the room at any time, it would test positive. The obvious question then being, did we want to just go ahead and process the room without the test and at least save the fifteen hundred dollars? I had to think a minute. Hmm. I said yes, of course.

Never saw anything like it. They came in, all suited up in white hazmat suits, respirators, gloves and booties. Every little thing—and I do mean everything— was wrapped in plastic, sealed in bags and taken out of the room. The furniture, the television, the fridge, the towels, the trash, the carpet, the light fixtures, the shutters, the guests' belongings, even the wallpaper. It looked like we had been visited by that little heartless green asshole Christmas thief on steroids. They then pressure-washed the tile and concrete floors. The entire contents of the room were loaded into a hazmat box truck and delivered to a special waste landfill to be appropriately disposed of. Well, that wasn't cheap.

To their credit, the company the Meth Heads worked for paid for the entire thing. They paid for the clean-up, they paid for the reconstruction of the room, they paid for every night the room was down during the two-month process. They apologized again and again. I don't know what for, but they did. It's not like they had "How to Build a Meth Lab" as part of their employee orientation training program. I let them know I understood that the Meth Heads' behavior was in no way a reflection of their business policies or practices and assured them that we would never let the newspaper know which company Meth Heads worked for.

After this, we instituted a brand new DND (Do Not Disturb) policy. One that protected our team, our customers and the hotel. Before, and as an industry standard, if someone had a DND sign on their door you didn't dare go in their room or knock on the door, no matter how many days it was on the door. Not after the Meth Head bullshit.

I not only changed the DND policy, it was printed on every registration card for the guests to sign. It read:

Every room will be entered daily regardless of DND status, for the safety and security of our guests, staff and facility.

You would be surprised by the number of people this would just piss the hell off, even after explaining the reasoning behind it. But you know what? I would much rather have had a few irked guests than dead ones. They would bitch to high heaven that they would never do anything, and profess that they had their right to privacy, blah, blah blah.

Well, wouldn't this just be a perfect fucking world? Maybe we should just do away with, let's say, the law against murder. What the hell? Most people are upstanding model citizens, and would never murder anyone, right? Or maybe we shouldn't have speed limits. After all, the greater part of mankind are damn good drivers. Oh, wait you mean these things are put into place to protect me against others, not myself? Wow, mind blown.

I am absolutely certain they would feel differently if their luggage was blown into the next county. Then they would be the first ones at my doorstep with their lawyers, wanting to know why I didn't do more to protect their whining ass.

It never failed; it always seemed like the guests that had the best jobs were the ones that had the most drugs. Like the "Because I Can" Man. Proving this theory once again, my head housekeeper, Erica, came to me one day and said her girls were having trouble getting in to clean a couple of rooms.

Erica, by all appearances, was quiet and focused. She, like all of us, had worked her way up to supervisor. I always had more confidence in her than she had in herself, and it was not misplaced or undeserved. Her worth was more than she allowed herself to own. She was thorough and conscientious and had a remarkable ability to sense when something just wasn't right. This time was a doozy and she wouldn't be wrong.

She let me know that both rooms were with the same company. One room never let them in or even answered the door and the other room would only open the door a crack. When they did, the girls saw towels stuffed to the base of the door. She told me they hadn't been able to get in the rooms since they checked in three days ago.

If you have ever worked in the hotel industry, you know that towels stuffed to the bottom of the door is never a good thing. Either it meant someone was trying to hide the fact that they were smoking in the room or your hotel was on fire. Since the sprinkler system and fire alarms had not gone off, my money was on the former. I looked at their information and they were all part of a crew there to work on cell phone towers.

Erica and I headed to the first room to clean it ourselves, thinking we were just going to find that they had been smoking and process it as such. She told me that she had seen them leave but needed a second supervisor to witness the incident report for the suspected smoking fee and I was the lucky wing man (or person). We knocked, announced ourselves and then used the master key to open the door.

Nothing seemed to be out of the ordinary and it didn't particularly smell like smoke. We walked around the room wondering why they wouldn't want housekeeping to come in. Then we saw it, but we didn't know what it was. These little grey green pieces of stuff on top of the desk. They were roughly the size of small marbles and course in texture.

At first, I thought, *Marijuana*. No, that wasn't it. Then I thought, *Mushrooms*. Nope, not that either. I didn't know what it was. I scooped it into an empty coffee cup and brought it down to the desk. I called the police to see if they would come take a look and maybe solve the mystery. When they arrived and looked at it, they had no idea either. They took it to the station to test it and would get back to me.

Meanwhile Erica and I headed to the second room, the crew leaders' room. He and his assistant were bunking together. I figured we would clean the room for the day ourselves. Same thing, knocked, announced, entered. At first glance, all seemed well. Suitcases about the room, damp towels on the floor, empty soda bottles on the dresser. It's funny how, when you take that cursory glance, everything seems fine and then your eyes and mind start to focus, and you home in on disturbing details. As my gaze travelled over the room, it came back to the open desk drawer. Needles, burnt spoons, lighters, tie-offs, foil packets. Holy crap; heroin. Not even hidden.

As I called the police, the details in the rest of the room started to paint a sinister picture. As fate would have it, I turned around and the police were at the door, cup in hand. The substance had tested positive as heroin. They told me they would need a search warrant to enter the room. I said I just might have something better than that.

The actual registered guest in the room was the company. I called the company and asked for a manager. The receptionist wanted to know what this was regarding. I thought this situation was way too messy to discuss with her, so I simply told her we were having a problem with their credit cards. I waited on a brief hold, going over the scene in the room to their classical hold music. It was kind of like replaying a mini modern-day opera in my head.

Soon enough, an unsuspecting cheerful manager answered the phone, oblivious to the fact that I was about to ruin her day. I gave her the short story of it and she confidently assured me that they drug tested all their crews on a regular basis because of the dangerous work they did. After all, they climbed cell towers for a living. Regardless of her argument, she gave their full permission to cooperate with the police in any way. I assured her I would call her with any updates.

Even the police could not believe the amount of heroin and paraphernalia in this room. It was everywhere; the desk drawer, the dresser, the nightstand, in every suitcase, stuffed up under the bathroom vanity; literally in every nook and cranny. There were hundreds of needles, cotton balls, and foil packets. There were clear plastic sports drink bottles full of piss, and miniature metal energy drink bottles with hand warmers around them, secured with electrical tape. All of this among their work laptops, climbing D rings, tools and pictures of their families.

I learned a lot that day. I learned that heroin is melted in a spoon and then sucked up through a cotton ball into the syringe before injecting it. That is what had turned those cotton balls into the grey green pieces of something we had found in the other room. They were the filters for the supervisor's heroin. He was giving his leftovers to his workers so when they had enough, they could put them together for a second hand high. Effectively, throwing them his scraps.

I learned that the girls we saw them take to their room peed in bottles for them and they poured it into the tiny energy drink bottles because they were small enough to hide in their pocket or tape to their leg. I learned that they taped the hand warmers to it to keep it body temperature warm. This way, when it was tested, it would be just right. I learned drug addicts don't like to do drugs alone. I learned drug addicts have good jobs and families and they don't give a shit about any of it.

I took pictures of the piss-filled plastic bottles and handwarmer-wrapped mini metal pee bottles and texted the pics to the company so they would know how their drug tests were being passed. The police dealt with the rest. The High Climbing supervisor came walking down the hallway and bolted when he saw the police. He ran to his company vehicle where the rest of the guys were and drove off, leaving his luggage, his family photos, his laptop, his tools and his stash. I wondered which one of those the High Climbers would miss the most.

The manager called a couple of days later wanting to know if any of the High Climbers had come back to the hotel, as they had not returned their company vehicle yet. I told her no, but we did have all their tools, computers and personal belongings. She apologized for everything that happened and let me know they would send someone to get everything. She thanked us for our diligence and let me know that because of what happened they were changing their drug testing policy.

I wanted to know something, though. How in the hell did they fly thousands of miles from home and get their hands on that much heroin or the ingredients for a meth lab in just a few days? I knew they didn't bring it through the airport, or hell, maybe they did, and I was just naive as hell. I mean, every time I flew, I got one of those little cards in my luggage that said my bag had been searched. The closest thing to drugs that I packed in my suitcase were the multitudes of stress reducing vitamins and herbal supplements I took.

This is what's wrong with our society today; everyone wants to medicate everything away. When did the world decide that everyone should be happy or numb all the damn time? That is not how life works.

You are supposed to grieve when someone dies, and it's supposed to hurt, and it's supposed to take a while to come to terms with it. You are supposed to be anxious or nervous when you're going into a job interview or the first day at a new school. You're supposed to be scared when you quit your job or file for divorce. You are supposed to be pissed or angry when someone cheats on you or insults you or your family. You're supposed to cry and be sad when your friend moves away or your pet dies.

These are called emotions, people, and, believe it or not, we are supposed to have them. The not-so-nice ones go hand in hand with the great ones, like love, laughter, joy, gratitude. Society has made it acceptable and expected to prefer to be legally medicated by doctors or illegally medicated by ourselves out of processing, embracing and getting through the tough times and bad shit. The world condones it and it's a damn shame.

Hell, even physical pain. You know I have had more surgeries than I would like to count and never took pain meds for more than two days out of hospital. You know why? Because pain is there for a reason. To tell my stubborn ass when to stop doing shit or that I am doing too much. We are not supposed to feel good or be pain-free all the time. Sorry to burst the rose-colored bubble, but the world needs to just grow the hell up.

And don't' start thinking, *Oh, she's just a small-town prude, goody two shoes, she doesn't know what it is like*. The hell I don't. Like almost anyone out there I have lost those I love to addiction and I have watched it tear my and other families apart. The disease debate is a muddled one at best. I am a firm believer that addiction starts out as a choice, not a disease—at least in the beginning.

In this day and age with all the education and information out there in every possible format, why the hell would someone even start that shit? What possessed them to stick that needle in their arm for the first time, take those pills, snort that powder? Then they're gone, or at least the person you knew is gone, lost to their demons, and it will be the fight of their life to escape them. I will not enable an addict, but I will love and support them when they are ready to stop. God knows they will need all the help they can get to do it.

Given my own life experiences with this subject, I hate to say that illegal drugs could actually be funny, but they can be, it's true.

We had—like all hotels—a lost and found department. Standard protocol was anything found in a room gets bagged and tagged. It's placed in a bag along with the date it was found, the room number it was found in and the name of the guest and the team member that found it. We did not call guests and notify them of their forgotten item. Why not, you ask?

Let's talk this one out, shall we? Me: "Hello this is Tammy from the hotel, and I was just calling to let you know that John left his shirt and a dress here during your stay last night."

Wife: "I didn't spend the night at a hotel last night, so why would there be a dress?"

Oh Shit. Fight! Is he cheating on her, is he a closet transvestite, what? Divorce, our Fault. Nope, not making that phone call.

The only things we didn't put in lost and found were items that would spoil, items of a sexual nature, (gross, and please refer to previous chapter on sex), anything breathing, or any illegal substances. Customers would call for their left-over food and be pissed we didn't save their scraps or the two cans of beer they had left in their fridge after checking out, even though all their other belongings were gone. Half a cheeseburger, two slices of pizza or a couple of beers have never been as valuable as when someone left them in their room and one of our team members had thrown them away.

I never had anyone call for the sex toys or porn. Thank God. As I finish this statement, I am in complete and utter fear that just because I have now written these words down and put them out into the universe, I will get a phone call or email in the near future, from one of my many Service Warrior friends still safe behind their counters, relating a guests' request for the prompt return of their adult supplementary sex shit.

Big shock, guests would come back for their drugs. This would be right up there with forgetting sex toys, guns and porn. How do you forget your stash? I believe doing so would lend itself to the intelligence of a drug addict. Coming down off their high, and needing another one, they realize, "Shit! Where did I put that?"

They would return to the hotel and approach the desk, obviously agitated, asking for a key to the room they had already been checked out of and that had subsequently been cleaned. This meant that we had found and subsequently confiscated their stash and turned it over to the local police to be properly disposed of.

To their great dismay, we wouldn't give them a key because it was well past check-out time and the room was then clean. They would demand a key. We'd ask why they needed the key. They'd say they left something important in their room but never wanted to say what that important something was. I loved this part. Honest, it was one of my favorite scripts of all time and I never got tired of reciting it. I'd tell them, with a smile and as politely as if I was giving someone directions to the local church, "Oh yes, we found what you left in your room and turned it over to the local police department for safekeeping."

I would then hand them the phone number to the local police station and let them know that if they would like to claim their lost item, the police would be more than happy to assist them in any way that they could. Bahahaha! This is where the laugh-until-you-cry emoji would be. They would leave, thoroughly pissed, and yet I was completely and utterly amused.

Short excerpt: One morning I was in the office at the little forty-unit mom-and-pop, when a housekeeper called me to a room because she found a bag filled with small white rock-looking things. I told her not to touch anything, that I'd be right there, and hung up the phone. I called the police and printed a copy of the guest info before I even left the office. By the time I got to the room outside, the officer was just rolling up. It was a cop I knew. We had graduated high school together and he was one of those guys I was utterly shocked had become a high-

and-tight cop and totally upstanding member of society. As per our high school experience, he could have gone either way.

Exchanging pleasantries, I followed him through the open door of the room. The housekeeper was making the bed and she stood up and pointed towards the microwave. Sure, enough, a sandwich-size plastic baggie full of small white rocks was sitting on top of the white microwave. There was nothing else left in the room. The room wasn't left a mess; there was no damage, just a large bag of crack. The Forget Me Nots had checked out early that morning and left their precious package behind.

The information on file was not helpful. The reservation had come through a third party, they were from Washington, had stayed only the one night, were in a rental car, and there was no way of knowing where they were headed. We did know one thing, though. At some point that day, someone was going to be really, really, really pissed off. The smirking officer took it with him, along with their info— you know, just in case they called. I told him that if we heard from the Forget Me Nots, we would send them his way. We both walked out of that room having a pretty good day.

Then there were the customers I was genuinely forced to assume were high simply because of the silly stubborn shit that spilled out of their mouths. The ones that made me wonder, *How stupid are you?* This is a true story, I swear. At the front desk we were routinely questioned, mostly by touristy guests, "What brings people to this area?" Which translated to the real question, which they were either too afraid or too polite to ask: "Why the hell are there so many hotels here and, why do people come to this godforsaken place?"

My standard response was always the four C's: Copper, Cotton, Cattle and Convicts. (That last one we just didn't put on the billboards.) The next most often-asked question was, "What is growing in the fields we passed?" This usually happened in the early fall when the cotton had flowered with its beautiful yellow blooms.

One time, Becki and I were at the desk checking guests in, and a very nice, well-spoken woman, about our age, asked that very question. Becki, who was entering the lady's credit card information, casually replied, "Cotton." The woman promptly told her she was wrong. With that, Becki looked up and said, "No, really, it's cotton." The lady again, more emphatically, told her she was wrong. The Cotton Queen assured us that she was from Texas and she knew what cotton looked like and that was most certainly not cotton. Becki tried once more, and I tried backing her up by chiming in to the affirmative. Becki tried letting her know that she had been born and raised here and that it was cotton. The lady was having none of it. She insisted, in no uncertain terms, unequivocally, that that was not cotton growing in those fields.

The Cotton Queen snagged up her keys and marched off to her room, confident she was right, and thoroughly annoyed that we did not know any better and could not answer her question. Becki and I looked at each other and Becki asked me, "Was she high?"

What the hell was someone supposed to think? You asked

a question, we gave you the goddamn answer, and then you proceeded to repeatedly insist we were wrong. Well, if she was so damn smart, why did she ask the question in the first place?? Honest, we had lived here if not all, most of, our lives. We knew what the hell they were growing in the fields. It was cotton!!!! I figured the Cotton Queen was possibly growing some other type of flowering plant at her place back in Texas and she'd been smoking a little too much of it, resulting in the diminished brain cells she had on full display.

There was no more perfect storm than the combination of a drunk-ass guest and an inanely clueless customer service representative. We had promoted a front desk attendant to front desk supervisor at one of our properties. She was ex-military, friendly, responsible, disciplined and detail oriented. I would add that she was an independent problem solver, but in this story that was not a plus. Let's just say she was high strung and High and Tight.

Over a weekend, High and Tight worked the night audit shift at one of the hotels because a team member had called in sick. There were a couple dozen rooms full of boisterous work crews and a number of rooms in-house for a lovely wedding at the local Mormon temple, including the grandparents of the bride. A diverse group, in both purpose and partaking.

Around midnight, guests from both groups started straggling in, some from a cider-sipping reception and others from a party where they slammed—not sipped—a little harder fare. One Slammer was noticeably soused, slurring his speech and unsteady in his step. Wobbly, he headed to his room with the rest of his crew. Everyone went to bed and High and Tight went about her duties.

About an hour later, Slammer must have gotten thirsty or hungry, as he was up and about trying to get something out of the vending machines on the second floor. This would have been all well and good, but in his drunken state, he could not accomplish the task of putting the coins in that little itty-bitty slot. In his urgency to quench his craving he also thought it unnecessary to put any clothes on before leaving his room. He was at the vending machines stark naked.

One of the signs of obvious intoxication is losing inhibitions. Given Slammer was out in the hallway naked we can check that box. Another is the urgent need to pee, which he also had and proceeded to relieve himself right there in the corner between the vending machines and the elevator. Check. (Thank God we had tile floors.)

It just so happened the elevator door opened mid-stream and it was our freshly promoted High and Tight supervisor, who was innocently doing her rounds and slipping that lovely receipt under everyone's doors. Nothing like the overspray of piss and the sight of a naked man to shake up your night. Slammer didn't miss a lick and completely unfazed, finished his business. Undaunted High and Tight approached him, and in no uncertain terms, ordered him back to his room. A fuzzy confused look is all she got in return, and he made no effort to cover himself or leave the elevator area.

High and Tight thought she could handle him and the awkward, bordering on illegal, situation and went back down to her post at the desk. Confidently she grabbed a couple of bath towels and made Slammer a room key. Despite seeing him in a whole different light she was secure in the knowledge that she knew what room he was in and convinced she could handle this lewd lush. She went back upstairs, and Slammer was proudly standing over his puddle of piss, mumbling to the vending machines. Fearlessly, High and Tight wrapped a towel around him and guided him to his room, opened the door, and nudged him through it. All was well except she still had to clean up his body fluid-ridden mess. Which, to her credit, she did.

All was well. All was well. All was well. Just three innocent little words. It never ceased to amaze me how just three little words could screw with a person when you let them creep into your well-intentioned mind: *"Internal Revenue Service, I love you, I hate you, I have protection, This won't hurt."* I had thought *All was well* many a time throughout my career and when I did it never failed to motivate the universe to unleash her sense of humor.

Everything would have been fine if High and Tight had been correct about Slammers' room number, but she wasn't. She had broken one hard-and-fast, sound as steel, never wavering, rule of hospitality. Never, never, never let someone into a room or make them a key without seeing their picture ID and verifying they are a guest of that room. There were absolutely no exceptions to this rule, ever. High and Tight broke this rule in every way possible. Slammer was too drunk to give her his name or room number and too naked to be carrying ID.

Our saving grace was that the room she did shove Slammer into was at least that of another crew member, instead of the sweet, unsuspecting, temple-worthy grandma and grandpa. The fellow crew member hadn't been much better off when he went to bed and didn't notice Slammer until he woke up the next morning. Not to say he wasn't perplexed and pissed that he woke up with a naked man in his room, but it could have been so much worse. That scenario is what my nightmares were made of.

High and Tight would lose her job over that one, and rightfully so. She never called me and asked what to do, she never called her supervisor and asked what to do, she never called the police and asked what to do. She wasn't afraid to call either, because she would call for stupid boring shit like a missing credit card authorization or a room move, but a drunk and disorientated naked man pissing in the hallway, she mistakenly thought, *I got this*.

CHAPTER 16

DECENCY TO THE RESCUE

(SUITE KNIGHTS ABOUND)

If you have been lucky enough or cursed enough, depending on how you look at it, to make any form of customer service your career, whether temporary or permanent, you have been trained. Trained how to apologize, whether you mean it or not, trained to listen attentively and feign concern. You have had every style and mode of mantra shoved down your throat by an overenthusiastic albeit well-intentioned mentor or supervisor.

You sit and listen with an attentive nod and the occasional yawn, and wish you could ask them instead, "This is great and all, but how do I handle the man, who, just yesterday, shrieked I was a worthless inept bitch because he wanted his burger and French fries both fresh? And when the fries came out fifteen seconds before the burger, he then wanted new fries when I put the burger on the tray, because now the fries were no longer fresh. Then, when the new fries came out, he wanted a new burger because now the burger wasn't fresh."

That is what we all really want to know.

By the way, I was an unfortunate exasperated witness to this frustrating scenario as my husband and I waited in line at a fast food burger joint in Scottsdale, Arizona. I thought the twenty-something, putting-herself-through-college young lady was going to cry when this entitled, khaki-clad, Jesus-shoe-wearing, OCD jackass did this. To my husband's credit, he restrained himself from exercising his fatherly instincts. I saw it though, sitting there in the tense squaring of his jaw, the deep furrowing of his brow, and the pursing of his lips. His hands were thrust deep in his pockets as if they would keep him from grabbing this guy by the scruff of the neck.

In the nick of time, OCD Jackass's food was finally and simultaneously fresh enough, and he proudly took his tray to a table. When it was our turn to order, I loudly told the obviously shaken girl how beautifully she had handled the situation and praised her self-control. With a mother's wisdom fortified with years of experience, I let her know that she didn't have to take that type of abuse. She nervously thanked us for our encouraging words and told us it was her first week on the job.

I didn't like it at all. I saw myself in her flustered smile and her shaking hands, and I just wanted to give her a hug and tell her that not all workdays would be like that. Some would, but not all. (If anyone knows me, I am not a hugger. I don't like people I don't know very well in my space. I hug those I love, thank you very much.) This girl reminded me of a younger me, before I figured out how to value myself. I hurt for her because I knew she had taken his words to heart. She would go home focusing on his rant, and not on all the other great people she had waited on that day, (like us). Do you think there was a manager to be found? Someone to come to her defense and throw that OCD Jackass out like he deserved? Hell no.

The poor girl had a shitty customer and a shitty supervisor. We have all been witness to this, even outside our own businesses and jobs. Supervisors cowing down to the customer and not taking a stand when they really needed to. Step it up people; when will management learn to value their teams? If they don't, when and how will shitty customers learn to behave?

During Christmas shopping season I was guaranteed one miserably inevitable annual ordeal. Everyone knew it was going to happen. Standing in a long, agonizing line at the local big box toy store. So why did people bitch about the wait, and make rude, snarky little comments, not quite under their breath, about whoever the poor bugger was unlucky enough to be working the register? And there would always be, The Instigator. The one who would get just a little louder each time they added a jab to their childish rant, rallying the troops of fellow stressed-out holiday shoppers into their rank and file of dissatisfaction.

Personally, I loved to hear those swelling tides of impatient shoppers, as they tried to suck everyone around them into their two-sizes-too-small of a heart, with their two-sizes-too-big of a mouth. Not me, I would not let them dismantle my holiday spirit or demean the dedicated holiday helpers. I offered a pleasant smile and would say loudly and with a little chuckle, "I know what you mean, but it could be worse; you could work here and have to listen to people complain about something you can do nothing about."

The persecuted cashier would offer up a thankful smile and a grateful nod. The rank and file and The Instigator would suddenly have an *Ah Hah, I was being an asshole moment,* and become much more amiable. The conversations would turn to lighter things and more appreciation would be shown to the tense overworked cashier. Did anyone really think they were going in and getting out in under fifteen minutes? If you are going to be an ass about waiting, stay home and shop online.

One-night Eric and I had taken my mom and our whole fam-damly out for dinner. Table for six, please. My dad was doing an overnight in the hospital after receiving numbers twelve through fifteen heart stents. (No, I did not make a mistake in those numbers.) It had already been a trying day and we just wanted to have a peaceful meal and sink into a mentally exhausted sleep.

We picked a franchised family style restaurant not far from our hotel and were greeted by a gracious host and promptly seated. Our waitress was a jovial young lady, with a pleasant smile and an accommodating demeanor. She recited the night's specials and took our drink orders. While she was away, they seated an elderly man at the table just behind my husband and me. He looked to be a proper gentleman. His crisply pressed white shirt and trousers along with his freshly cut hair and straining suspenders whispered of a bygone era. An era where manners were taught and expected. This would not be the case.

As she walked past Bygone Era to deliver our drinks, she acknowledged him with a cheery greeting and let him know she would be right there. Expertly, she balanced her tray and placed our drinks in front of us and, with pen and pad in hand, asked us if we were ready to order. Bygone Era interrupted her and gruffly asked if she was going to take care of him. Upon hearing that, we told her to go ahead and take care of him; we would wait. Who knows maybe he was a diabetic and needed to eat or something. At least that would have explained his hateful mood.

Retaining her good nature, she promptly turned her attention to Bygone Era and recited her specials and asked for his drink order. He skipped over the drink part and gave her his entire order. She thanked him and then turned her attention back to our table. We gave her our order and she thanked us and left to enter the orders. In a matter of a few minutes she returned with his beverage, which was ice water, and baskets of warm bread and whipped butter for both tables. She told us all she would be back in a jiff with our soups and salads, and she was off, stopping to check on a couple of her other tables on the way back to the waitress station.

Shortly after her departure, Bygone Era flagged down a passing server. He reported that he had specifically asked for a little ice in his water and the girl had put too much and his water was now too cold to drink. The unsuspecting server picked up his glass and said she would take care of it. With this second, more-rude-than-the-first, interaction, I was now intently interested and listening.

Our steadfastly cheery server made her way to our tables with a large tray containing our soups and salads. She served the gentleman first and gave him a fresh glass of water, which had just a few ice cubes in it, and apologized. Again, she turned her attention to our table and served our plates. Before she could pick up her now-empty tray, he caught her attention again. This time to say there was now too little ice in his glass of water and to inform her that light ice was not that difficult of a concept to master.

She apologized again, took his glass and returned with a brilliant solution. She brought a bowl of ice, a small pitcher of water and an empty glass. I thought, *Well played seasoned Service Warrior, well played. Problem solved.* You'd think. Instead he berated her for expecting him to make his own glass of water. He informed her that if he had wanted to do that, he would have stayed home. Without hesitation and with an unwavering smile she spooned ice cubes into his glass until he said stop and then filled the glass with water.

Now that Bygone Era had treated us all to a modern-day version of *The Three Bears* and his water was now just right, I hoped the rest of the evening would be peaceful. Wrong. He had ordered the special, just like three of us had at our table: beef tips and gravy, garlic mashed potatoes and green beans.

Our meals all came out at the same time and the girl cleared our array of empty salad plates and soup bowls. She let us know she would be back with refills of our beverages.

Pitchers in hand she returned to our table. Soda for the kiddos, tea for the adults and more tepid water and fresh ice cubes for Bygone Era. As she poured our drinks, she asked us how everything was. We let her know everything was great. And it was. The specials were especially good. I know this because we are one of those families where everyone tries to order something different so we can all try a little bit of everything.

You would think since three specials were perfectly wonderful at our table that Bygone Era's meal might be as well. Sadly, this would not be the case. Nothing was right—too much gravy on his potatoes, mashed potatoes were too lumpy, beef was too tough, green beans were too bland. With each new grating insult or complaint, my ire was raised to a new level. To her credit, our stressed-out server handled it beautifully, apologizing and offering a new meal, which he refused. It was odd. For someone so unhappy with his meal, Bygone Era cleaned his plate.

After getting no bites for dessert, she brought our ticket and offered to take it to the cashier when we were ready. As she went to process our ticket, Bygone Era stopped our server and asked to speak to the manager. She asked if there was anything she could do, and he firmly said no and demanded to speak to the manager. With that she was gone.

The manager returned, who, it turned out, was the pleasant

gentleman who had seated all of us. He asked what he could do. Bygone Era was on a tirade. Not yelling, not cussing, just a brutal, unfounded tirade about how inept the server was and how much worse the food was. He went on and on with completely unnecessary insults about the server, who we knew had tried so hard to please him. Without noting the now-empty, nearly-licked-clean plate; without taking leave to speak with his well-trained server or his proficient kitchen crew, the manager offered to comp Bygone Era's meal.

We couldn't believe our ears. What was he doing—or better yet, what *wasn't* he doing? The young lady had done nothing wrong. In fact, she was a model of customer service, the food was more than palatable—it was great—and the customer had finished it all. The manager turned around and left to go take care of this jackass's ticket.

I couldn't help myself. I got up and followed him, stopping him half-way to the register. I told him he was wrong. I told him his server had gone above and beyond the call of duty and that the food, which we all had as well, was wonderful. I told him how Bygone Era had treated his server. I asked him not to comp that man's meal, that he didn't deserve it. If anything, that man had ruined our and everyone else's dining experience. The manager just looked at me with that customer service guru blank stare.

Finally, when he woke up from his dose of reality haze, he apologized to me and said it wasn't up to him. The owner abided by a strict no-bad-review policy. In other words, if a customer complained, it was comped. Period. I couldn't believe it. This spineless corporate foodie establishment was going to comp Bygone Era's meal, even though his shitty attitude ruined other patrons' experiences. No questions asked. They were going to let their server feel undervalued by going undefended and untipped, all to save a possible bad review from a horrible guest. Fine then.

Disgusted and disappointed I headed back to our table to gather my things and my family. My dear husband could tell I was upset, and, to his credit, his attitude wasn't too far behind mine. A sting of apprehension came over me when I saw my husband stop at Bygone Era's table on the way out, as I knew how protective he could be. That soon disappeared when I heard him respectfully preach a little to that man.

Given Bygone Era's age, my husband politely introduced himself and courteously offered his hand. The man met the gesture with a firm but softer grasp. Calmly my husband said, "Sir I sat here all evening with my family and was waited on by the same girl and ate the same food, and you know, the only thing that ruined my meal was having to listen to how you treated that young lady. She was nothing but kind to you. I don't know if you just had a bad day or if you're just mad at the world. Doesn't matter. She didn't deserve the things you said to her or about her. Now I am leaving with my family and I am going to leave that girl a good tip for having to put up with you, and I hope you do the same and I pray you have a better day."

Now ask me why I love that man? He was just as upset, maybe even more so yet he remained respectful and polite and was a shining example of consideration, kindness and, frankly, self-control for me, for our kids, for our server, for that spineless manager and, most of all, for Bygone Era.

On occasion our chivalrous customers would come to the rescue of one of our own. We had a lovely young lady, Amber, who worked the night or graveyard shift at our front desk, and I knew it took an immense amount of strength to put herself out there. She had a medical condition where she had lost most of her hair and she was very self-conscious about it. Regardless of her insecurity regarding her hair, she was an outgoing and friendly personality behind the counter and always worked very hard and took great pride in looking her best.

I identified with her vulnerability. I remembered how I felt after my accident, how unsure of myself I had been and what it took to put myself out there. As a company we wanted to help and had given her the money for a wig that she had wanted. Not that she needed it, as she was a beautiful soul with or without it.

One night a customer came back to the hotel, drunk and hungry. He wanted something from the vending machine before heading to bed. Fumbling through inserting the money and selecting his option, he was frustrated when the money got stuck. When shaking and beating the machine failed to produce his treat, he headed to the front desk, still drunk, mad and looking for a target. There was Amber.

She offered Drunk and Disorderly his money back, but he didn't want it. He wanted his snack, and when she couldn't do that, she became the object of his vicious attention. He yelled at her that she wasn't fooling anybody with her pathetic comb over, that no one would ever think she was pretty, that she was disgusting and ugly. She started to cry, and with that, he was satisfied and stormed off to his room.

She never called me; she never told his boss. She pushed it down, she swallowed it as if it was okay, as if she somehow deserved it. I thank God her incoming relief for the next shift knew there was something wrong when they saw her. Amber told her relief that something had happened but wouldn't elaborate. When I came in, the relief told me what she knew, that she was concerned for her co-worker, and showed me the communication log where Amber requested to work at one of the other hotels. That request and the relief's concern echoed in my mind, as I called Amber and asked what had happened. With a cracking voice that I recognized all too well, she told me the story. My heart broke for her. I told her I would take care of it, and, by God, I was going to.

I knew the crew Drunk and Disorderly worked with and I knew their boss. They had always been nothing but respectful. By the time I came in the crew had already left the hotel for work that day, but they would be back, and I would be there. To facilitate a speedy solution to the issue, I called the Boss Man and told him what had happened and informed him that Drunk and Disorderly could no longer stay at the hotel. Boss Man was mortified, and I understood why. His own wife had recently been struggling with losing her hair due to chemo treatments. Now it was my turn to be reassured that it would be taken care of.

Within an hour Boss Man, Drunk and Disorderly and their entire crew were in the lobby of the hotel. Boss Man sent two of his crew members with Drunk and Disorderly to help pack his stuff, and the rest of the crew took seats in the lobby. Boss Man apologized and let me know that Drunk and Disorderly would be taken home to Phoenix and would no longer be working with them. I told him that he had nothing to apologize for, that I knew he nor his crew were represented by the actions of this one man. (Wait, "man" is too good of a word. Let's see, maybe narcissistic sadistic abusive jackass. Yes, that would be better.) The crew all gave affirming nods in my direction.

The ding of the elevator bell was like the ringing in of a boxing round. The crew all stood up with arms crossed, facing the desk. With Boss Man standing between the elevator and the crew, they formed an intimidating escort. Drunk and Disorderly stopped at the desk and sheepishly offered an apology and told me he would like to apologize to Amber in person. I told him that while I would relay his sentiment, he didn't deserve to speak with her, that his apology would only unburden his mind. Nothing he could now say would erase what he had said to her. He couldn't unsay it, she couldn't unhear it, and for her, it would not be easily forgotten.

The crew stood there as silent guardians as Drunk and Disorderly was escorted to his waiting ride. We never saw him again and every one of the other crew members made a point to speak to, encourage and compliment Amber. She may not have been able to forget his words, but they were drowned out and overshadowed by the fierce loyalty and chivalry of true roughneck gentlemen. They served to restore her and my faith.

Being a decent human being doesn't just refer to how we treat others but how we treat ourselves as well. When pulling these stories out of my customer service-traumatized psyche and assembling them for this book, I found that there were thousands of books out there on how to provide excellent customer service, what it means, and blah blah blah, and even more on how to be a better, more authentic self.

I am sorry, there are not thousands of different ways to do this shit. For how you treat others, no matter which side of the counter you stand on, there is one rule and one rule only, and I have never understood why it is so damn hard to live and work by; the Golden Rule, when it applies. I don't know if it is funny or sad that the "Treat others how you wish to be treated" rule we never manage to apply to ourselves. I mean why don't we treat ourselves better. We are taught in customer service to value everyone around us, but not ourselves. We learn that we are only valued as part of a team that is there to please the customer at any cost.

I believe this is partly why I found it so hard to jump off the pages of my well-scripted life. It was ingrained in me from the age of ten that I was there to make everyone around me happy—the customers and my parents, at any cost. I chased paper to hang on my wall, but it was to my parents' end. It was where I felt safe, it was where I grew up, regardless of the decades of verbal abuse, regardless of successes or failures. It was who I was; the ever-pleasing service warrior and, hardworking serial entrepreneur,

Now with the encouragement of those I fortified through the years, I have garnered the courage to walk away from that script and write my own story. I am scared, just as I should be. It is fascinating to look to my future and realize I can do whatever I want. I can write my books, I can tell my stories, I can un-script my life, and I will be okay—and so will those around me.

My adventure began in the pages of this book and I pray you laughed and cried with me. I aspired to anger and inspire you. I hope you recognized a part of yourself hidden among these words. I will be deeply gratified if some Gypsy Princess buys it to use the pages to wipe her more money than sense, college educated, expanded vocabulary ridden ass. I did it and at the end of the day I am now the person I want to spend the rest of my life with.

CHAPTER 17

How to Be a Good Customer

(Or better yet; just how to be a decent fucking human being.)

This chapter isn't even a chapter, rather just the sharing of my short and Suite, hard earned wisdom.

Is the customer, always right? As per the writing of this book...Fuck No! God, I wish this was an audio book, because the anguish and satisfaction in which that phrase would be screamed would be gut-wrenchingly satisfying. But there was not one book I could find on what you should do or how you should go about being a good customer.

What is a good customer? It's someone we all want to help and do our best for. Because they make us feel good when we do our job to the best of our ability and they appreciate it;

not with insincere gushing, just by treating us with respect, by complaining constructively when needed, and having a smidgeon of patience. I beg, on behalf of Service Warriors everywhere, take my stories and advice to heart. It really is that easy; apply common sense, complain constructively and be kind. And remember if you can't be nice, at least:

DON'T BE A DICK!

If you cannot refrain from being a dick, no matter how hard you try, and this book has not served to change your ways, then by all means, do us all a favor and either bless the doorstep of our competition or:

FUCK OFF!

WHO THE HECK IS TAMMY?

Tammy was raised in the hospitality business. By the age of ten she was helping her parents with their first motel, working housekeeping, laundry, front desk, maintenance and switchboard.

After a devastating accident as a teen, Tammy found solace in books and music. Instead of following her passions, she spent four decades in family businesses. Twelve years as operations manager of their multi-state waste management company while taking care of the roadside hotel and family diner. Eventually she jumped back into the family business of hospitality, managing four hotels, a multi-screen entertainment center, a restaurant and saloon, a retail floral and gift shop, a convention center, a miniature golf and sports park, and ultimately owning two hotels of her own.

Tammy spent twenty years pursuing validation on paper, earning her Bookkeeping Certificate, and an AAS degree in Business Admin. She became a Certified General Manager and a Certified Hotel Administrator, an MSHA Instructor, a tax specialist and a certified master florist.

Newly retired, from running someone else's dream, Tammy is taking on the world in different ways; books, speaking engagements and inspiring everyone to "embrace the chaos" and "un-script their life." Having broken the chains of serial entrepreneurship Tammy enjoys cooking, planning road trips with her husband and three amazing children, cultivating new adventures, writing and listening to good music.

Read more about Tammy at:
www.tammymayhew.com
www.facebook.com/TammyMayhewAuthor

Made in the USA
Las Vegas, NV
26 May 2021